Controlling Bureaucracies

Controlling Bureaucracies

Dilemmas in Democratic Governance

JUDITH E. GRUBER

UNIVERSITY OF CALIFORNIA PRESS
Berkeley   Los Angeles   London

University of California Press
Berkeley and Los Angeles, California

University of California Press, Ltd.
London, England

© 1987 by
The Regents of the University of California

Printed in the United States of America

1 2 3 4 5 6 7 8 9

Library of Congress Cataloging-in-Publication Data

Gruber, Judith E.
Controlling bureaucracies.

Includes index.
1. Bureaucracy.   2. Bureaucracy—United States.
3. Democracy.   I. Title.
JF1507.G78   1987   350'.001   86-6935
ISBN 0-520-05646-9 (alk. paper)

For Samson

Contents

Preface

Finishing this manuscript has taken me from one side of the continent to the other. Along the way I have accumulated a significant number of debts that I am delighted to be able to acknowledge.

Funding for the early stages of the research was provided by the National Institute of Mental Health. The writing was supported by the American Association of University Women and, at the University of California, Berkeley, by the Institute of Governmental Studies and a Robson fellowship from the Department of Political Science. I am very grateful to all of these institutions for making an often painful process at least relatively painless financially.

This book obviously could not have been completed without the cooperation of its subjects: the thirty-nine administrators in education, fire, and housing. These men and women generously gave me their time and tirelessly answered my questions. I learned a tremendous amount from them not only about the problem of democratic control but also about the delivery of local services. My only regret is that insurance regulations prevented me from learning how to slide down a fire pole.

My greatest intellectual debts are to my teachers, colleagues, and friends. Douglas Rae, more than anyone, taught me how to think analytically. Edward Pauly and Douglas Yates first encouraged me to pursue the problem of bureaucratic responsiveness and provided invaluable guidance throughout the project. Numerous other friends and colleagues assisted me at critical points along the way. I am particularly grateful to Patricia Brown, Karen Christensen, Judith de Neufville, Robert Lane, David Lapin, William Muir, Kathy Roper, Eleanor Swift, Jerry Webman, and two anonymous readers for the University of California Press, each of whom managed to provide precisely the help I needed at the time I needed it. Jennifer Hochschild and Janet Weiss provided more help than any friend or colleague could hope to receive.

I had two institutional homes while I worked on the research for this book. The first was the Institution for Social and Policy Studies at Yale University. While I was there, Charles E. Lindblom created an enormously stimulating intellectual environment that aided my work in subtle, but important, ways. While Ed Lindblom himself has not read the manuscript, I am nonetheless grateful to him because his example sharpened the quality, if not the specific substance, of my thinking. More recently, the Department of Political Science at the University of California, Berkeley, brought me to the beautiful Bay Area, where I found many distractions but also a fertile intellectual environment for finishing this work.

Finally, there is my family. I come from a home where work and marriage are joined, and I have to remind myself how unusual it is to receive love and professional help from the same source. My parents support each other personally and professionally, and they have also always done the same for me. They gently goaded me to finish my work by clearly reserving a place on a bookshelf for it. They also provided considerable help: I probably have the best-educated newspaper clippers and proofreaders in America.

My marriage, happily, is no less extraordinary than that of my parents, and my greatest debt of all is to my husband, Joseph Houska. I have read many acknowledgments trying to figure out how to thank him, and nothing seems adequate. He cajoled when I needed cajoling; he harangued when I needed haranguing; he encouraged when I needed encouraging. But he did much more than that. Every time I got into an intellectual thicket, he helped me out of it by talking through the ideas until they made sense. Every time a chapter seemed in danger of drowning in metaphors and convoluted prose, he rescued it. This book would not only have been much weaker without his help, it might not have been at all.

1
CONTROLLING
BUREAUCRACIES

We live in a democracy. That fact, taught in school and persistently reinforced by political oratory, is a source of pride and satisfaction to most of us. Although we often disagree about what a democracy entails, most people would probably accept the idea that the heart of a democratic political system is control of the government by the governed. In modern, complex democracies complete control is, of course, impossible, but at minimum we expect the popular election of public officials.[1] Americans are particularly fond of using elections to keep public officials accountable. While the turnout for American elections is smaller than in many democracies, the number of officials we elect is large.

We also live in an increasingly bureaucratized society. Large organizations—corporations, unions, merchandising chains—play a growing role in our lives. So, too, do large government agencies. Almost one-fifth of working people in this country are government employees, and in spite of our propensity for elections, only a tiny fraction

---

1. Robert A. Dahl, *Dilemmas of Pluralist Democracy* (New Haven: Yale University Press, 1982).

of these are elected officials.[2] The public official a citizen is most likely to encounter is not a legislator, mayor, governor, or president, but a bureaucrat—an IRS agent, an administrator in the motor vehicles bureau, a welfare worker, or an agricultural extension agent.

As almost anyone can testify, these bureaucrats do much more than the proverbial paper pushing. They routinely make decisions that significantly affect the way government serves or regulates its citizens. Congress may pass the tax code, but an IRS agent decides whether a specific individual's expenses qualify as deductions. A state legislature may enact a program designed to improve the basic skills of students, but state administrators decide which particular programs and which particular schools are eligible for funds. A city council may pass a rent control ordinance, but local bureaucrats decide whether the improvements an individual landlord has made mean that rents for individual tenants may be raised. Although the impact of each of these decisions may be small, collectively they determine the texture of the relationship between citizens and government.[3]

Bureaucrats have not usurped this power from elected officials; they have been given it deliberately. Congress would be crippled if it had to decide on each citizen's taxes, as would city councils if they had to assess all rents. State legislators rarely have the expertise to evaluate individual educational programs. Elected officials have nei-

2. U.S. Department of Commerce, Bureau of the Census, *Statistical Abstract of the United States 1982–3* (Washington DC: Government Printing Office, 1982), p. 394.

3. Michael Lipsky argues that "there are many contexts in which the latitude of those charged with carrying out policy is so substantial that studies of implementation should be turned on their heads. In these cases policy is effectively 'made' by the people who implement it." (Lipsky, "Standing the Study of Public Policy Implementation on Its Head," in Walter Dean Burnham and Martha Wagner Weinberg, eds., *American Politics and Public Policy* [Cambridge MA: MIT Press, 1978], p. 397).

ther the time nor the specialized competence to make such decisions. These officials choose to delegate power to bureaucrats both for reasons of efficiency and to take advantage of the professional competence many bureaucrats possess.

Yet the result of such delegation is that the people making the myriad decisions about who benefits and who is regulated are not voted in and out of office by the citizens they are benefiting and regulating. They are generally people hired on the basis of competitive examinations, promoted on the basis of the judgments of other bureaucrats, and fired only under extreme provocation. How then is their work to be controlled by ordinary people? How can we reconcile the growth of decision making in powerful government bureaucracies with our ideas of democracy and popular control?

Current political debate testifies to the seriousness with which some view the problem. A central question in many political campaigns has been which candidate can best grapple with the bureaucracy. Over a decade ago an unsuccessful presidential aspirant mobilized his supporters by decrying bureaucrats in Washington who carried nothing more in their attaché cases than their lunches. More recently, presidential candidates have waged successful campaigns running as Washington outsiders unbeholden to entrenched bureaucratic interests and therefore allegedly better able to control them. Once in office most successful candidates have discovered that the problem is more formidable than they thought. Merely announcing a change in marching orders is rarely enough to shift markedly the direction of the tens of thousands of bureaucrats who control the day-to-day operation of government agencies and who possess both the information and the expertise necessary to make those agencies work.

The need to control bureaucracies is a problem that

crosses many political boundaries. Officials trying to cut back the scope of government activity can find themselves frustrated by bureaucratic inertia, as happened to the Nixon administration in its efforts to reduce public welfare expenditures. High-level officials found themselves unable to stem burgeoning spending because bureaucrats in the then Department of Health, Education, and Welfare were unwilling to monitor and limit the activities of the state and county officials whose programs were fueling the budgetary fires through federal matching provisions.[4] Leaders who seek to expand or change the scope of government action can find themselves equally frustrated. For example, when the New York City Board of Education sought to increase integration through policies such as open enrollment and comprehensive high schools, it was hindered by the refusal of bureaucrats to disseminate information about the options to parents and to design new curricula.[5]

Neither is the problem of governing bureaucracies limited to the United States. Ezra Suleiman describes the French bureaucracy as "accused of technocratic power and arrogance, of bureaucratic highhandedness and inefficiency . . . and of constituting a closed and a ruling class."[6] In Great Britain Michael Gordon finds civil servants whose influence "is hardly confined to an administrative exercise" and who "may even determine the ultimate success of the party's program."[7] Throughout the Western world elected officials find themselves depen-

4. Richard P. Nathan, *The Plot That Failed* (New York: John Wiley and Sons, 1975), p. 84.

5. David Rogers, *110 Livingston Street* (New York: Random House, Vintage Books, 1968), chap. 8.

6. Ezra N. Suleiman, *Politics, Power and Bureaucracy in France* (Princeton: Princeton University Press, 1974), pp. 30–31.

7. Michael R. Gordon, "Civil Servants, Politicians, and Parties," *Comparative Politics* 4 (1971): 41–42.

dent upon appointed ones to achieve their political ends. The challenge for these officials is to find sensitive and nuanced ways to control bureaucrats without losing the benefits that bureaucratic action brings.

Control of large bureaucratic organizations is not a problem unique to democratic political systems. Leaders of large corporations and heads of nondemocratic nations also find themselves confronting bureaucrats who are not always pliable. Corporate leaders, for example, may find their efforts to computerize company finances thwarted by the persistence of an accounting department in conducting its business by hand. Military governors trying to change the regional distribution of public services may be no more able to alter established bureaucratic patterns than their democratically elected counterparts.

Controlling bureaucracies, however, takes on special urgency in democracies because unaccountable power flies in the face of the central norms of such political systems. When the legitimacy of a government derives from the consent of the governed, the problem becomes not merely an inability to get the governmental apparatus to act in ways the leaders or citizens wish but also a challenge to the fundamental nature of that government.

Early analysts of administration did not see the reconciliation of democracy and bureaucracy as a problem. They accepted, at least in principle, the Weberian description of the impersonal bureaucrat working with equal diligence for a succession of masters.[8] Writers such as Frank Goodnow and Woodrow Wilson believed that the administrative realm of the bureaucrat could be separated from the political or policy-making functions of legislators and

---

8. H. H. Gerth and C. Wright Mills, *From Max Weber* (New York: Oxford University Press, 1946), pp. 228–29.

elected executives.[9] Democratic control of appointed administrators was assured through their subservience to elected officials.

Of course, such a neat compartmentalization of government functions is illusory. A dichotomy between policy and administration may be a comfort to those fearful of bureaucracy's undemocratic features, but it is not an accurate description of reality. In the course of making their decisions about how a program will actually work, bureaucrats give that program shape and form. They are guided by the decisions of legislatures, but those decisions often do little more than establish a broad domain within which bureaucrats must act. Carl Friedrich summarized this less tidy view by asserting, "Public policy, to put it flatly, is a continuous process, the formulation of which is inseparable from its execution."[10]

More recently, scholars have explicitly compared bureaucrats and politicians in terms of their political beliefs and their contributions to the policy process. They have found that though the process may be continuous, these two sets of political actors do play different roles.[11] The resurrected distinction between bureaucrats and politicians is not, however, one in which the former passively serve the latter. Rather it is one in which politicians and bureaucrats bring distinctive perspectives and competencies to policy making.

9. Frank J. Goodnow, *Politics and Administration* (New York: Macmillan, 1900), and Woodrow Wilson, "The Study of Administration," *Political Science Quarterly* 56 (1941): 481–506.

10. Carl J. Friedrich, "Public Policy and the Nature of Administrative Responsibility," in C. J. Friedrich and Edward Mason, *Public Policy 1940* (Cambridge MA: Harvard University Press, 1940), p. 6.

11. Joel D. Aberbach, Robert D. Putnam, and Bert A. Rockman, *Bureaucrats and Politicians in Western Democracies* (Cambridge MA: Harvard University Press, 1981).

The problem of control thus remains, and the question recurs, What methods can be used to govern policy makers in public bureaucracies democratically? The early architects of our political system, although greatly concerned with avoiding tyranny, gave little thought to the problem. As Peter Blau explains, "Our democratic institutions originated at a time when bureaucracies were in a rudimentary stage and hence are not designed to cope with their control. To extend these institutions by developing democratic methods for governing bureaucracies is, perhaps, the crucial problem of our age."[12] Unfortunately, it is a problem for which there is no single solution.

Perhaps because our political institutions were not designed at a time when large, powerful bureaucracies were prevalent, efforts to control them have been varied, but not systematic. The Constitution makes little mention of the bureaucracy; its only requirement is that the president appoint the heads of the executive departments with the advice and consent of the Senate. Our federal system of government has allowed the individual states to experiment with their own modes of controlling bureaucracy. Political executives, legislative oversight, administrative courts, advisory boards, review boards, ombudsmen, ethics legislation, community control, "sunshine" laws, and many other tactics have been touted and tried as means of control. But the choice of a specific control mechanism often seems to depend more on political fads than on careful assessment of the relative merits of various possibilities. Debate over methods, in both the political and the scholarly arena, generally has an ad hoc quality, with the focus on the effectiveness of specific procedures, not

12. Peter M. Blau, *The Dynamics of Bureaucracy* (Chicago: University of Chicago Press, 1963), p. 265.

on how diverse control mechanisms affect the overall problem of reconciling bureaucracy and democracy.

The language used to discuss democratic control complicates efforts at more general appraisal because that language is capable of many interpretations. Everyone, for example, wants a "responsive" school bureaucracy, but what they want may vary considerably. For parents it may mean administrators who consult them on curricular issues, for teachers it may mean a system that applies due process criteria to all personnel decisions, and for the mayor it may mean a superintendent who coordinates school policies with those of other city agencies.

Such ambiguity hides substantially different analyses of the problem of bureaucratic control. As James Q. Wilson has noted, "There is not one bureaucracy problem, there are several, and the solution to each is in some degree incompatible with the solution to every other."[13] For the parents in the example above, the bureaucracy problem lies in the procedures school administrators use to reach decisions. For the teachers, the problem lies in the capriciousness of the results of decision making. And for the mayor, the problem lies in the fragmentation of bureaucratic decision making. Each actor sees controlling bureaucracies as a way of achieving a different political value, and each actor would go about pursuing control in a somewhat different fashion.

Access, fairness, coordination, and many other goals are all desirable for a democratically controlled bureaucracy, but they are by no means the same, nor always compatible. Reforms aimed at realizing one value may impair our ability to realize others. An agency that treats all citizens identically is not likely to be one that responds flexibly to variations in citizen needs. Communities that in-

---

13. James Q. Wilson, "The Bureaucracy Problem," *Public Interest* 6 (1967): 4.

troduce procedures that create a permanent record every
time a police officer's radar gun clocks a speeding vehicle
do so in order to prevent the unfairness that is created
when police ignore violations by prominent officials or by
people who offer them bribes. These same procedures,
however, make it impossible for the police to overlook
someone speeding a sick friend to the hospital.[14] Similarly, the centralized control needed to increase coordination may directly conflict with the decentralization dic-
tated by the aim of reducing bureaucratic insulation.
Creating regional offices of federal agencies may effectively improve contact between bureaucrats and the citizens they are serving, but it may make it more difficult
for agencies to ensure that their various activities work in
harmony.[15]

Debate about democratic control of administration is
further clouded by disagreement about what *democracy*
means, and hence about what it means to control a bureaucracy democratically. Perhaps because the claim is so
desirable, advocates use the adjective *democratic* to describe a host of institutional arrangements.[16] Some of
these arrangements are designed to secure the liberties

14. Jerry L. Mashaw explicitly discusses the consistency/flexibility trade-off
in terms of disability decision making in his *Bureaucratic Justice* (New Haven:
Yale University Press, 1983), pp. 86–87. Eugene Bardach and Robert A. Kagan
discuss it in terms of the problem of regulatory unreasonableness in their *Going
by the Book* (Philadelphia: Temple University Press, 1982).

15. A. H. Birch, writing not about bureaucracy but about the more general
issue of "responsible" government, detects similar confusions and conflicts of
meaning. He uncovers three meanings for the concept "responsible": responsiveness, consistency, and accountability. "Responsiveness and consistency are
desirable ends that are wholly compatible only in rare combinations of circumstances. Accountability is not an end in itself so much as a means whereby one
or (to some extent) both of the other ends may be secured (Birch, *Representative
and Responsible Government* [London: George Allen and Unwin, 1964], p. 131).

16. C. L. Stevenson discusses words like "democracy" that "have both a
vague conceptual meaning and a rich emotive meaning. The conceptual meaning of them all is subject to constant redefinition. The words are prizes which
each man seeks to bestow on the qualities of his own choice" (Charles Leslie
Stevenson, "Persuasive Definitions," *Mind* 47 [1938]: 333).

of the citizenry, some to ensure that government achieves the wishes of the citizenry. Some arrangements emphasize the role of groups in government, others the role of individuals. Proponents of each arrangement allege that it furthers the goal of democracy, but the characteristics of that goal are quite diverse.

When the element of control is added to the concept of democracy, the waters become still murkier. Some bureaucratic reforms have been proposed in the interests of democracy that in fact have little to do with control. The suggestion that public agencies should be staffed by individuals representative of the general population is an example.[17] To the extent that such staffing policies provide a weak form of control by the groups the administrators are representatives of, they indeed are an example of democratic control. However, arguments for such staffing patterns are often made in the interests of fairness or of making people feel closer to their rulers. Such goals may be important for a democracy, but they are not the same as democratic control. Similarly, some have seen democratizing the internal workings of an agency as an important component of a reconciliation of democracy and bureaucracy.[18] Internal democracy is not, however, a means of democratic control and in fact may provide a serious impediment to the exercise of such control by substituting self-rule for popular rule.[19]

17. This position typifies what has been called the representative bureaucracy approach to public administration. See, for example, J. Donald Kingsley, *Representative Bureaucracy* (Yellow Springs OH: Antioch Press, 1944), and Samuel Krislov, *Representative Bureaucracy* (Englewood Cliffs NJ: Prentice-Hall, 1974). Frederick C. Mosher takes a similar position when he argues that the educational channels to administrative jobs should be open to all segments of society (*Democracy and the Public Service* [New York: Oxford University Press, 1968], chap. 2 and pp. 215–19).

18. See, for example, Warren G. Bennis and Philip E. Slater, *The Temporary Society* (New York: Harper Colophon, 1969).

19. On this issue, see, for example, Blau, *Dynamics of Bureaucracy*, pp. 264–65; M. R. Godine, *The Labor Problem in the Public Service* (Cambridge MA: Har-

If we are to be selective about where the laurels of democratic control are bestowed and clearer about the kinds of choices we make when we choose a means of control, we must consider all control mechanisms together. Looked at singly, the details of a given plan stand out. Looked at together, the contours of the problem stand in relief. To see these contours we need a map showing the various possible routes to the goal of a democratically controlled bureaucracy.

BUREAUCRATIC DEMOCRACY

Bureaucracies pose a problem for democracy when they make governmental decisions—that is, public policy—and thereby short-circuit electoral channels of public control. Electoral controls themselves may not always be effective, but short circuits in them further increase the potential for significant governmental actions to be taken in the name of the public without being influenced by the public. This problem is lessened, or avoided, if the range of acceptable bureaucratic behavior is in some way limited or constrained so that the public exerts control over decision making. Hence, the idea of constraint is the essential component of all mechanisms to be included in my map.[20]

Defining the problem as one of constraint allows us to cast a wide net, a net that catches most of the ways the issue has typically been discussed. Accountability, responsibility, and responsiveness all imply setting some limits on bureaucratic behavior.[21] What varies is which aspects

---

vard University Press, 1951), pp. 45–51; or Peter M. Blau and W. Richard Scott, *Formal Organizations* (London: Routledge and Kegan Paul, 1963), p. 55.

20. Herbert J. Spiro, writing about bureaucratic accountability, similarly argues that the goal of restraint is common to all views of accountability (Spiro, *Responsibility in Government* [New York: Van Nostrand Reinhold, 1969], p. 98).

21. A. H. Birch distinguishes three ways for popular control to be exercised: through advance instruction, via post accountability, or by means of com-

of bureaucratic behavior are constrained, and how tightly. Is the constraint the relatively loose requirement that administrators "respond" to the needs of the people, or the tighter one inherent in precise legislative formulas for the distribution of funds? Does the constraint center on prohibiting corruption or favoritism, or does it entail specifying the goals or policies the bureaucrats must pursue?

All behavior is in some way constrained, of course, whether by the values of an individual actor, by the resources that actor has available, or by formal limits on what may be done. What transforms constraint into democratic control is its imposition by a democratic political actor—either the citizens or their elected representatives. This may be done by citizens acting alone or in groups, by elected legislators or executives. It may be done directly through command or indirectly through an intermediary such as a politically appointed executive. It may be done negatively through sanctions against certain forms of action or positively through incentives to behave in specified ways. All that is essential for my purposes is that a mechanism impose constraint on bureaucratic behavior, that it be legal, and that the constraint be directly traceable to the citizenry.

The last condition is crucial. Mere congruence of bureaucratic action with citizen wants does not constitute control. If by happy coincidence bureaucrats act the way citizens want them to, bureaucracy may seem to be less of a problem, but it is not under democratic control.[22] As

---

petition of elites. All of these applied to the bureaucratic arena involve a degree of constraint, if only that indirectly imposed by an elected official who is eventually held responsible for the actions of bureaucrats in his or her administration (Birch, *Representation* [London: Pall Mall Press, 1971], pp. 112–14).

22. For a discussion of the problematic relationship between the actions of democratic political institutions and the achievement of citizen wants, see Douglas W. Rae, "Political Democracy as a Property of Political Institutions," *American Political Science Review* 65 (1971), pp. 111–19.

Robert Dahl explains, control is "a relation among actors such that the preferences, desires, or intentions of one or more actors bring about conforming actions, or predispositions to act, of one or more other actors. Control is thus a causal relationship: the actions of one actor are interpreted as having been brought about, or caused by, the preferences of other actors."[23] Without the hand of the citizen, democratic control of bureaucracy does not take place.

Control may occur through a process of anticipated reactions. If bureaucrats accurately anticipate what the hand of the citizen would do, and then feel constrained to act on the basis of that anticipation, a form of democratic control has occurred.[24] If the bureaucrats are wrong in their anticipation and act in ways the citizenry or legislature does not approve of, however, it cannot be said that their actions have been controlled by the citizenry.

IDEALIZED PERSPECTIVES

Two basic aspects of bureaucratic behavior may be subject to constraint: the procedures used to make decisions and the substance of the decisions actually made. Procedurally, an administrator may be required to hold hearings, to consult certain groups before taking action, or to hire personnel in a prescribed fashion. Substantively, the administrator may be limited, for example, to making de-

---

24. As Dahl explains, "control need not be intentional; it may also be unintentional. Although Beta's action *x* must be brought about by Alpha's preferences, desires, or intentions, Alpha need not specifically desire or *intend* that Beta do *x*. What is crucial is that Alpha wants *x* to occur (or wants the results of *x*), and that, as a result, Beta does *x*" (Dahl, *Dilemmas*, p. 17).

cisions that serve to increase the amount of rice produced in the country or that provide low-cost housing for the elderly.[25]

The distinction is not absolute. "Procedure" and "substance" are in part determined contextually. The holding of public hearings may at one and the same time be the process by which decisions are made and the substantive result of an earlier decision about how to proceed. Procedure may also be a determinant of substance. The way a decision is made can significantly influence it. Nonetheless, the distinction is both heuristically useful and practically applicable. Every decision has both a procedural aspect and a substantive component. Either or both may be constrained through specific control mechanisms.

Constraints do not merely exist or not exist; they can be imposed in varying degrees. The more constrained behavior is, the smaller the range of permissible alternatives open to the bureaucrat—that is, the less his or her discretion. A central point of contention among theorists and practitioners concerned with reconciling bureaucracy and democracy has been just how much discretion a bureaucrat should have. It was a major issue in the early colloquy between Carl Friedrich and Herman Finer on the nature of administrative responsibility.[26] It remains

---

25. Other analysts have used similar distinctions to characterize a variety of political phenomena. Hanna Fenichel Pitkin describes both formal and substantive approaches to representation. The former are concerned with institutions and rules; the latter focus on purpose, intention, and motive (Pitkin, *The Concept of Representation* [Berkeley and Los Angeles: University of California Press, 1972], p. 238). Joseph Tussman argues that there are "two great moods of deliberative life," the purposive and the casuistic, or legal (Tussman, *Obligation and the Body Politic* [New York: Oxford University Press, 1974], p. 86). While realizing that "the interplay of purpose and law . . . is constant," Tussman nonetheless is able to "imagine a scale or spectrum marked at one end 'rule dominated' and at the other end 'purpose dominated'" and then to locate tribunals on the scale.

26. Friedrich, "Public Policy," p. 6; Herman Finer, "Administrative Responsibility in Democratic Government," *Public Administration Review* 1 (1941): 335–50.

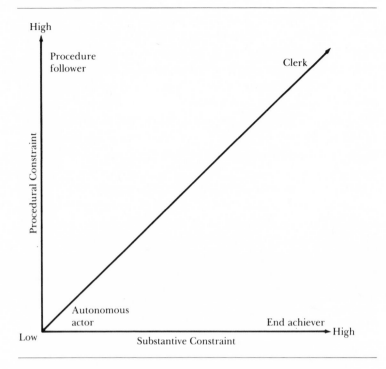

Figure 1. Idealized Perspectives of Bureaucratic
Democracy

an essential difference among proposals for bureaucratic
control today.

Control mechanisms are located on the map, then, on
the basis of two variables: the degree to which the mechanism constrains bureaucratic behavior and whether it is
the procedure by which bureaucrats make decisions or
the substance of those decisions that is constrained. The
borders of the map consist of two axes—procedural constraint and substantive constraint—with each varying
from low to high. (See Fig. 1.)

Before going on, two things should be stressed. First,
this is a map of mechanisms for democratic control of

bureaucracy, not a map of all the ways bureaucratic behavior may be constrained. Some mechanisms that in fact tightly constrain the behavior of bureaucrats do not appear on the map because the constraint does not derive from the citizens. For example, virtually all bureaucrats are constrained by the abilities of the people working for them and the limited capacity of complex organizations to harness those abilities. These constraints are a form of democratic control only insofar as they are a product of public pressures or decisions.

Second, discussions of more or less constraint should not be interpreted as discussions of more or less democracy. Whenever constraint is exerted by the citizens or their representatives, some degree of democratic control of bureaucracy exists. As I argue in chapter 2, however, whether that control is sufficient depends on one's definition of democracy. Fairly weak forms of control are congruent with some theories of democracy, but barely acceptable to others. Various positions on the map should therefore be interpreted as representing different, but not necessarily more or less, democratic visions of how a bureaucracy should be controlled.

Situated in the corners of the map are four idealized perspectives on how bureaucrats should behave in a democracy. Since they represent extreme cases, these perspectives are rarely, if ever, reflected in specific control mechanisms. Understanding them does, however, help to locate actually occurring proposals on the map and to clarify relationships among them.

In the lower left-hand corner, where both procedure and substance are very loosely constrained, is the bureaucrat as autonomous actor. Such a bureaucrat's actions may be competent, professional, and otherwise satisfactory to the citizenry, but they primarily result from his or her choice and not the choice of the citizens.

Diagonally opposite the autonomous actor is the dem-

ocratically controlled bureaucrat as clerk. Here, both procedure and substance are so tightly constrained as to leave
the administrator no discretion at all. It is this vision that
formed the basis of the old, extreme, and now largely
discredited view that policy and administration are separable, and hence that all administrative action flows directly from democratically made legislative decisions. In
caricature, the job of the bureaucrat is to determine what
situation he or she is faced with and then to administer
the "correct" treatment that has been previously determined by elected officials.

The upper left-hand corner of the map represents the
situation where procedural constraint is high and substantive constraint is extremely low. This describes the bureaucrat as procedure follower. The orientation reflected
here focuses on the importance of due process to the exclusion of other concerns. Bureaucratic decision making
is considered consonant with democracy as long as closely
specified procedures are followed; the substance of the
decisions is left to the discretion of the bureaucrats.

In the lower right-hand corner is the democratic bureaucrat as end achiever. In this case, the substance of
decisions is highly constrained, the procedures not at all.
The bureaucrat's role is to secure publicly specified goals
using whatever procedures he or she thinks best to reach
those goals.[27]

APPROACHES TO DEMOCRATIC CONTROL

These four cases define schematically how bureaucratic
behavior may be constrained, and hence democratically

27. A. D. Lindsay expresses this vision as follows: "Government [is] . . .
given a free hand to deal with means. The purpose of the control exercised by
the ordinary voters is to see that those means—the technical skill of the administrative—are used to the right ends" (Lindsay, *The Modern Democratic State*
[London: Oxford University Press, 1969], p. 276).

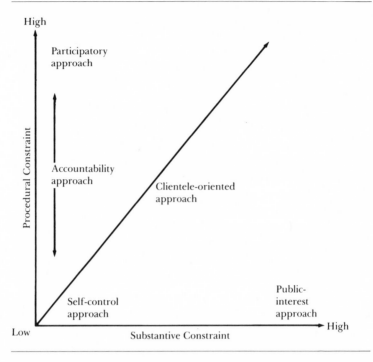

Figure 2. Approaches to Democratic Control

controlled. In the space between them we can locate various specific proposals arising both in social science literature and in popular discourse. I have grouped commonly occurring proposals into five broad approaches to democratic control: (1) control through participation, (2) control through clientele relations, (3) control through pursuit of the public interest, (4) control through accountability, and (5) self-control. Each of these approaches occupies a portion of the map, although the specific features of any given control strategy determine its exact placement. (See Fig. 2.) Each approach implies a different perspective on why we need to control bureaucracies and on how to go about doing it.[28]

1. Participatory control lies near the top of the map where procedural constraint is high. According to proponents of this approach, the problem with public bureaucracies is that they are isolated from the public, and hence are closed, undemocratic institutions. To counteract isolation, highly constraining procedural changes, such as community participation requirements, are advocated. All such changes center on increasing direct citizen involvement in decision making.[29] Many control mechanisms have participatory elements, but for those that lie in this region of the map participatory decision making is itself the goal. Many advocates of participatory reform assume that these changes will also produce change in the nature of policies, and hence substantive constraint. However, since the essence of participatory reform lies in changing the way decisions are made, substantive constraint is ancillary.[30] Constraining procedures to increase the citizen role does not inherently imply con-

28. There are parallels between these approaches and those several other scholars have suggested. Douglas Yates contrasts two models of bureaucracy, an administrative efficiency model and a pluralist model. The former, based on Woodrow Wilson's ideas about neutral competence, is similar to my approach of self-control; the latter is similar to the clientele approach (Yates, *Bureaucratic Democracy* [Cambridge MA: Harvard University Press, 1982], chap. 2). Jerry Mashaw describes three models for administrative justice: bureaucratic rationality, professional treatment and moral judgment. The first emphasizes the accurate realization of legislative will and is a cousin of the public interest approach discussed below. The second emphasizes the appropriate use of professional expertise and is cousin to self-control. The third emphasizes the fairness of the process through which decisions are arrived at and is cousin to the accountability approach (Mashaw, *Bureaucratic Justice*, chap. 2).

29. Authors such as Milton Kotler, *Neighborhood Government* (Indianapolis: Bobbs-Merrill, 1969), and Marilyn Gittell, *Participants and Participation* (New York: Praeger, 1967), are typical of this perspective.

30. This point is made by L. Harmon Zeigler and M. Kent Jennings, *Governing American Schools: Political Interaction in Local School Districts* (North Scituate MA: Duxbury Press, 1974), pp. 8–9.

straining substance as well, and certainly not constraining it in a predictable way.

2. Clientele-oriented proposals, in contrast to participatory ones, are more concerned with the substance of decisions made in administrative agencies than with the procedural fact that they are made solely by administrators. Public agencies are seen as being undemocratic because their decisions inadequately serve the needs of citizens.[31] This substantive orientation is, however, linked to a procedural diagnosis of the problem—insufficient communication between bureaucrats and their clients. The clientele-oriented approach thus occupies a position near the center of the map, where both procedure and substance are moderately constrained. Constraint is moderate because advocates of this approach seek input and guidance from clients, not strict specification of action. Procedure is constrained primarily through requirements that administrators consult representatives of the groups most affected by the decisions being made, generally through advisory groups or panels.[32] Such consultation differs from that sought by advocates of participatory control in that the latter value involvement for its own sake, whereas clientele-oriented strategists seek more limited agency-citizen contacts to transmit information about the needs and values of client groups. By the same token, since the consultation is designed pre-

31. Herbert Kaufman describes this approach (*Red Tape* [Washington DC: Brookings Institution, 1977], pp. 47–48). Philip Selznick, *TVA and the Grass Roots* (New York: Harper and Row, 1966), H. George Frederickson, "Toward a New Public Administration," in Frank Marini, ed., *Toward a New Public Administration* (Scranton PA: Chandler, 1971); Avery Leiserson, *Administrative Regulation* (Chicago: University of Chicago Press, 1942); and David B. Truman, *The Governmental Process* (New York: Knopf, 1951), pp. 457–67, are among the authors who fall within this perspective.

32. Unfortunately, how to determine which groups are affected (or, for that matter, who should participate in the previous approach) is rarely specified clearly.

cisely to produce substantive changes in agency policy, clientele-oriented strategies are more substantively constraining than participatory ones.

3. In contrast, what I call the public-interest approach to democratic control is predicated on the assumption that, far from being inadequate, contact between bureaucrats and individual citizens or group representatives is pervasive. Policies emanating from bureaucracies are seen as fragmented or overly geared to the interests of particular groups. For proponents of the public-interest approach, the hallmark of a democratically controlled bureaucracy is that its decisions serve collective interests. In Sheldon Wolin's words, "'Political' responsibility has meaning only in terms of a general constituency, and no manipulation of fragmentary constituencies will provide a substitute."[33] The public-interest approach is oriented almost entirely toward constraining the substantive aspects of bureaucratic behavior, and therefore lies near the lower right-hand corner of the map. Advocates of this approach presume that elected officials will act to further more general interests (though of course in practice they often do not). Control mechanisms revolve around ways of increasing the reach of these officials into bureaucracies, making bureaucrats more responsive to the expressed policy initiatives of elected officials.[34] A moderate form of this approach is reflected in efforts to increase the number of political executives in administrative agen-

33. Sheldon Wolin, *Politics and Vision* (Boston: Little, Brown, 1960), p. 433. Other representatives of this approach include Theodore J. Lowi, *The End of Liberalism* (New York: Norton, 1969), and Mosher, *Democracy and the Public Service*, especially pp. 165–75.

34. Proponents of this perspective have almost always written about bureaucracies on the national level, but a comparable position could be taken from the perspective of states or cities. In that case emphasis would be placed on meeting statewide or citywide needs, and the desired responsiveness would be to governors and state legislators or mayors and city council members.

cies because these executives serve as conduits for the
substantive decisions of elected presidents, governors,
and mayors.[35] It is also reflected in line-item budgeting
designed to allow elected officials to direct how money
should be spent. A stronger manifestation is the advocacy
of decreased bureaucratic discretion through increased
substantive decision making by Congress and other legislative bodies, including those at the neighborhood
level.[36]

4. Procedure, not substance, is the focus of the accountability approach.[37] These proposals lie in a vertical
band on the left of the map, where procedural constraint
runs from moderate to high and substantive constraint is
low. The emphasis on procedure derives from the diagnosis that bureaucracies threaten democracy when they
abuse their power by acting corruptly, inefficiently, or un-
fairly. Procedural safeguards, or limits, are therefore advocated to ensure that such abuses do not take place.
These constraints are generally directed only at limited
aspects of agency behavior and are therefore usually less
constraining than participatory reforms aimed at changing the fundamental processes through which agencies
reach their decisions. Accountability mechanisms include
codes of ethics, civil service systems, and hearing and notification requirements. They also include reforms aimed
at facilitating the review of agency decision making such
as freedom of information acts, ombudsmen, and oversight boards. All of these focus on guaranteeing that de-

35. Mosher, *Democracy and the Public Service*.
36. Lowi, *The End of Liberalism*. For discussions of neighborhood based "legislatures," see Robert K. Yin and Douglas Yates, *Street-Level Governments* (Lexington MA: Lexington Books, 1975).
37. Authors who have written in this tradition include: Finer, "Administrative Responsibility"; Joseph P. Harris, *Congressional Control of Administration*
(Washington DC: Brookings Institution, 1964); and Walter Gellhorn, *When
Americans Complain* (Cambridge MA: Harvard University Press, 1966).

cisions are made in an "appropriate" fashion, with only peripheral concern for what the decisions are.[38]

5. Finally, there are those who say democratic control lies primarily with the administrators themselves. This approach of self-control is based on weak, usually indirectly imposed, external controls, and it therefore lies near the lower left-hand corner of the map. A mild form of this perspective is found among those who believe that control emerges from a process in which bureaucrats discern the limits of behavior the public will tolerate and then act within those limits. Proponents of a stronger, and therefore less constraining, form of this perspective assert that bureaucrats must serve the public, but that often they alone are in the best position to determine how to do so. In fact, for these people many more "political" forms of control work against the goal of public control.[39] For them, democracy is achieved by relying on bureaucrats' professionalism,[40] their sense of personal fulfillment,[41] or their background.[42] Many of these mechanisms, however, verge so closely on complete self-control that they scarcely lie within the borders of our map.[43] They may represent ways to achieve goals desirable in a democracy, but that does not make them democratic con-

38. For a discussion of the argument that accountability need not always imply substantive responsiveness, see Michael A. Baer, "Interest Groups and Accountability: An Incompatible Pair," in Scott Greer, Ronald D. Hedlund, and James L. Gibson, eds., *Accountability in Urban Society: Public Agencies Under Fire* (Beverly Hills CA: Sage Publications, 1978), pp. 217–23.

39. This argument is discussed by Martin Meyerson and Edward C. Banfield, *Politics, Planning and the Public Interest* (New York: Free Press, 1955), pp. 38–39n.

40. Friedrich, "Public Policy," pp. 12–14.

41. Stephen K. Bailey, "Ethics and the Public Service," in Roscoe Martin, ed., *Public Administration and Democracy* (Syracuse NY: Syracuse University Press, 1965), pp. 283–98.

42. Kingsley, *Representative Bureaucracy*, chap. 12.

43. See, for example, Suleiman, *Politics, Power and Bureaucracy in France*, p. 158, for a critique of the reliance on "representative" background characteristics as a means of securing a democratic administration.

trol. For even if the administrators in the end act in a way
consonant with citizen preferences, if the action is purely
at the behest of the administrators and not of the citizens,
democratic control has not occurred.

BUREAUCRATIC ATTITUDES

If the problem of reconciling bureaucracy with democracy ended with making an informed choice among various means of control, it would be complex, but, in the
end, fairly tractable. Bureaucracies are not abstract administrative structures, however, but agencies filled with
real people with their own interests and with considerable
resources to resist control when it does not mesh with
those interests. The exercise of control is therefore inevitably affected by those being controlled, the administrators themselves. The beliefs of these administrators, the
roles they play, the histories of their agencies, and the
resources they command all contribute to the way they
will respond to specific efforts at control. As a result, it is
crucial to understand the problem of democratic control
from the perspective of the bureaucrats as well.

Bureaucrats can respond to control in many ways. Ideally, they will accept it and act the way controllers wish
them to. They can, however, effectively hinder control. A
governor, for example, may seek through a politically appointed agency head to step up the enforcement of state
hazardous waste regulations, but if career administrators
oppose the governor's intervention, they may deliberately
slow down their investigations or do nothing to speed
them up.[44] Under other circumstances bureaucrats may

44. Donald P. Warwick argues that middle and low level administrators in
an agency "can protect their interests by tactics ranging from artful sabotage
to surface compliance" if they fail to "socialize" the agency head (Warwick, *A
Theory of Public Bureaucracy* [Cambridge MA: Harvard University Press, 1975],
p. 172).

accept the goals of a control-related reform, but not consider it a priority, and thus stymie the effort. For example,
a school decision-making structure may provide for consultation between administrators and parents, but administrators may fail to bring proposals to the parent group
consistently because of other demands on their time.

Democratic systems rely on the willing acceptance of
governmental procedures, and in this respect the influence bureaucrats have over control is but one example of
a more general problem democracies face. Robert Dahl
and Charles Lindblom argue that democratic structures
depend on

> the consciences, norms and habits of the people in the soci-
> ety, leaders and non-leaders alike. For it is these that define
> what uses of control are legitimate and what are illegitimate;
> what behavior is acceptable and what is not. And if these
> definitions, commands, permissions, and approvals pre-
> scribed by the norms, habits and consciences of the people
> are not appropriate to polyarchy, then no written constitu-
> tions, no guarantees, no prescribed codes, no laws will
> achieve it.[45]

Unfortunately the ubiquity of complaints about recalcitrant bureaucrats suggests that bureaucrats do not always
hold attitudes conducive to democratic control.[46] An appreciation of the bureaucratic perspective on control
should, however, help us understand when such acceptance will occur and how it may be achieved.

From the perspective of achieving democratic control,

---

45. Robert A. Dahl and Charles E. Lindblom, *Politics, Economics and Welfare*
(New York: Harper Torchbooks, 1953), pp. 287–88.

46. Recent cross-national research has found that bureaucrats hold quite
different political beliefs than politicians (Aberbach, Putnam, and Rockman,
Bureaucrats and Politicians). These findings suggest a further reason why bureaucratic attitudes may not easily coincide with political efforts at control and
thus why willing acceptance may be problematic.

all bureaucrats share the key characteristic of being appointed policy makers. But bureaucrats operate in a great variety of policy arenas, and it would be surprising if the attitudes of all bureaucrats were the same; it would also be surprising if we chose the same means of control for all of them. Citizens are likely to place much less value on flexibility, for example, in the nuclear regulatory arena than in the social services arena. Equally, the attitudes of highly professionalized NASA scientists are likely to be different from those of Social Security administrators. Thus a full understanding of the problem of controlling bureaucracies also requires an examination of the policy context in which control takes place.

I have begun to explore the problem of controlling bureaucracies by creating a common framework for assessing various methods of democratic control, a map in which proposed methods can be arrayed, and hence compared. Chapter 2 expands the framework by considering normative concerns. There I show how the instrumental question of the choice of a control mechanism is embedded in larger issues of democratic theory. In chapter 3 I turn to the question of the costs incurred by various forms of constraint.

Chapters 4, 5, and 6 introduce two complications to the choice among mechanisms to control bureaucracies: the attitudes of the bureaucrats being controlled and differences among the policy areas in which control takes place. In chapter 4 I switch perspectives from that of the democratic controller to that of the bureaucrat to explore how the problem of democratic control looks to them. On the basis of interviews with local administrators working in the fields of education, fire, and housing, I examine how bureaucrats see their own role in the policy-making process and how they reconcile resistance to external control with acceptance of democratic norms. In chapter 5 I begin the discussion of policy context by looking at how differences among policy areas may affect the values would-be controllers seek from control and affect the likelihood that the costs of control will in fact be incurred. In chapter 6 I extend the analysis of policy context by comparing how administrators working in different policy arenas view other political actors and hence the issue of control. Finally, in chapter 7 I leave the world of the bureaucrat and return to that of would-be controllers and discuss the lessons this research may teach them.

In sum, I seek to illuminate the general problem of how to impose democratic control on public administrators. To do this, I provide a structure for understanding the democratic values implicit in different means of exercising control and for evaluating the costs and benefits of various forms of democratic control. With this in hand, I don the lenses through which the administrators themselves view the problem of control. Together, the structure and the lens should aid us in understanding the choices, problems, and prospects of ensuring that our bureaucratic society remains democratic.

2

DEMOCRATIC BELIEFS: THE NORMATIVE DIMENSIONS OF CONTROL

A map has many uses besides aiding travelers in reaching their destination. It locates all destinations in relation to one another and thus gives the reader of the map a sense of the overall terrain. Similarly, our map gives us a way of grounding arguments about specific control mechanisms within a broader structure of analysis. By understanding how many of the attributes of particular proposals are linked to the positions they occupy on the map, we can generalize to classes of proposals and, more important, increase our understanding of the contours of the problem of democratic control.

In this chapter I connect control strategies lying in different territories of the map with beliefs about democracy. That such connections exist should not be surprising. At stake is how to control bureaucracy "democratically." Ideas about what democracy entails ought to play a prominent part in thinking about how bureaucratic decision making can be reconciled with democratic institutions.[1] This is not to say that normative debate

1. Hanna Fenichel Pitkin makes an analogous point about theories of representation: "In the broadest terms, the position a writer adopts within the

28

about bureaucratic control is in fact common. Quite the contrary is the case. But such debate is implicit in "pragmatic" discussions of what to do about the problem of bureaucracy.

An understanding of the normative issues embedded in the map provides a way of assessing control strategies by emphasizing the different goals for democratic control and the different visions of political actors embodied in them. It serves the further function of alerting us to the normative content of debate over various forms of control. Seemingly practical arguments may in fact be based on normative disagreements. The weaknesses of specific reforms may turn more on problems with underlying assumptions than on flaws in design. Attention to either of these phenomena may provide new interpretations of arguments raised about specific control strategies.

There is no neat typology of theories of democracy to provide a ready guide to the normative terrain. Partly this is because democratic theorists do not organize themselves into clearly identifiable camps. More important, it is because these theorists rarely deal with the problem of bureaucracy at all. It is generally ignored, assumed away by defining the role of administration as neutrally implementing legislative policy, or taken note of but dismissed. Direct application of theoretical orientations is often impossible, since the theories have been formulated without reference to the problems posed by bureaucracy. Robert Dahl, for example, both maintains that one of the eight conditions for polyarchal democracy is that "the orders of elected officials are executed" and realizes that this con-

---

limits set by the concept of representation will depend on his metapolitics—his broad conception of human nature, human society, and political life. His views on representation will not be arbitrarily chosen, but embedded in and dependent on the pattern of his political thought" (Pitkin, *The Concept of Representation* [Berkeley and Los Angeles: University of California Press, 1972], p. 167).

dition "is the source of serious difficulties," but then drops consideration of the issue entirely, saying that "the extent to which this condition is achieved is perhaps the most puzzling of all to measure objectively."[2]

Yet strong connections do exist between theories of democracy and strategies for bureaucratic control, particularly around two sets of normative issues. First is the debate over the relative capabilities of the rulers and the ruled. One's position on this issue conditions how tightly one believes bureaucrats should be constrained. Second is the broad question of what the proper role of democratic government should be, and, more specifically, whether government is valued more as a means for achieving substantive ends or as a set of procedures for safeguarding liberty. Different positions on this issue imply different kinds of constraints on bureaucracy. Together these two sets of issues provide the normative dimensions of the map.

THE RULERS AND THE RULED

At the heart of the first set of issues embedded in the map is the question, How capable are citizens of governing themselves? As defined in chapter 1, control of bureaucracy means removal of discretion from bureaucrats. This in turn requires the transfer of a measure of governmental decision-making power away from bureaucrats to the citizenry. But how great a transfer should occur? How much discretion should be removed? That depends on

2. Robert A. Dahl, *A Preface to Democratic Theory* (Chicago: University of Chicago Press, 1956), pp. 71, 73.

what one thinks about the ability of the people and of their elected officials to make governmental decisions.[3] Making governmental decisions involves choosing the courses of action government will pursue. How capable one thinks people are of making those choices depends in turn on how one thinks about political interests. Should we seek to have the expressed preferences of the citizens embodied in public policy, or is it better to respond to a more detached perception of public needs? Is it possible for an "outsider," be it a legislator or an administrator, to determine someone else's needs, or can needs only be known by the individual concerned? Are all preferences of equal value, or are there some that should be either inadmissible in government decision making or of particular weight?

Theorists have sought to determine the "right" answer to these and kindred questions, and many analysts have attempted to classify the possibilities.[4] For our purposes a precise categorization is not necessary. What is important is the basic relationship between the nature of interest and the ability of people for self-governance. The more one believes that government should respond not to what citizens say they want but to what decision makers think they need, or, quite distinctly, the more one believes that some wants are more deserving than others, the less

3. Other factors (such as the opportunity costs that the effort to control bureaucrats may extract) may, of course, enter into the choice of a control strategy in addition to the normative premises discussed here. See chapter 7 below.
4. See, for example, Brian Barry's distinction between want-regarding and ideal-regarding principles, and his discussion of the concept of interest in *Political Argument* (London: Routledge and Kegan Paul, 1965), especially chaps. 3 and 10; Charles E. Gilbert, "Operative Doctrines of Representation," *American Political Science Review* 62 (1963): 604–18; A. H. Birch, *Representation* (London: Pall Mall Press, 1971); Steven Lukes, *Power* (London: Macmillan, 1976); and Glendon Schubert, *The Public Interest* (Glencoe IL: Free Press, 1960).

one believes that the power of government should be
lodged directly and equally in the hands of the people.[5]

Modern democratic theory has typically examined political interests and citizen ability in the context of the relationship between voters and their representatives. The
growth of bureaucracy and the influence bureaucrats
have over the contents of policy decisions introduces a
new factor into the equation. The issue is not merely the
proper distribution of power between the rulers and the
ruled, but also the relationship between the rulers and
the ruled *together* on the one hand and the bureaucrats
on the other. Thus, the problem of how to control bureaucracy democratically in part hinges on the question,
How capable are the citizens *and* their elected leaders of
governing?

Answers to the classic question about citizen ability do
not automatically convert into answers to the variant that
includes bureaucrats. The belief that legislators are superior to citizens as governors does not necessarily translate into the belief that bureaucrats are superior to the
citizen-legislator combination. Traditional discussions of
the issue of citizen ability are not, however, irrelevant to
the problem of bureaucratic control. The arguments developed are highly instructive for the kinds of positions
that may be taken about the proper degree of bureaucratic discretion.

Barriers to Competence

By its very existence representative government signals at
least some limits on self-rule. The source of these limits,

5. Again, Pitkin's discussion of representation is parallel. "The more [a
writer] sees interests . . . as objective, as determinable by people other than the
one whose interest it is, the more possible it becomes for a representative to
further the interest of his constituents without consulting their wishes" (Pitkin,
Concept of Representation, p. 210).

more than their extent, is crucial for our consideration of bureaucratic control. We may think of two basic sets of barriers to self-rule: (1) structural barriers that derive from the complexity of the governmental process and (2) individual barriers that arise from putative shortcomings of the ordinary citizen. The two sets of barriers may co-exist and reinforce each other, but conceptually they are distinct and have quite different implications for bureaucratic discretion.

Information is the key to structural barriers: citizens are limited in the role they can play in government because they do not know enough. One reason they do not know enough is the sheer scale of government operations, or, as Walter Lippmann describes it, "the intricate business of framing laws and of administering them through several hundred thousand public officials."[6] A second reason they do not know enough is that they do not have the technical expertise needed to make sense of increasingly complex political issues. A. D. Lindsay explains, "We recognize that the man in the street cannot, in the strict sense of the word, govern a modern state. The ordinary person has not the knowledge, the judgment, or the skill to deal with the intricate problems which modern government involves."[7] Thus, one set of arguments we must consider is that the size and technical specialization of complex modern government combine to erect formidable barriers to the ruled also being able to rule.

A quite different set of reservations about the capabilities of ordinary citizens is based not on the challenge pre-

6. Walter Lippmann, *The Essential Lippmann* (New York: Random House, 1963), p. 110. Also see Joseph A. Schumpeter, *Capitalism, Socialism and Democracy* (New York: Harper and Row, 1962), pp. 256–64, for the argument that the distance between citizens and the problems governments must deal with makes ordinary people incapable of self-governance.
7. A. D. Lindsay, *The Modern Democratic State* (New York: Oxford University Press, 1962), p. 267.

sented by government complexity, but rather on an assessment of human nature. Although there are substantial variations in emphasis and nuance within this group of arguments, the basic theme is that what individuals think is best for themselves is not necessarily what is best for society. The challenge to citizen competence thus takes the form of questioning the very legitimacy of citizen rule. Leaders are needed to steer government onto the appropriate course, to save people from themselves.[8]

One strand of thinking ascribes the need for leadership to the instability of individual preferences and the inability of people to account for the ways in which their desires affect others. Unbridled citizen demands produce chaotic and ephemeral public policies. As A. H. Birch argues, there is a "gulf between the policies a government would follow if it responded to the varying day to day expressions of public opinion and those it must follow if its policies are to be coherent and mutually consistent."[9] For government leaders to act responsibly, they must temper the pursuit of popular wishes with a measure of wisdom.

A second variation on the theme of the need for leadership suggests that individual preferences not only fail to produce responsible collective action, they are often not even reflections of true needs. From this perspective it is the pursuit of the latter that is the proper role of government.[10] Joseph Tussman writes, "Government is purposive, but it is a mistake to suppose that its purpose

8. Peter Bachrach characterizes such arguments as elite theories. He argues: "All elite theories are founded on two basic assumptions: first, that the masses are inherently incompetent, and second, that they are, at best, pliable, inert stuff or, at worst, aroused, unruly creatures possessing an insatiable proclivity to undermine both culture and liberty" (Bachrach, *The Theory of Democratic Elitism* [Boston: Little, Brown, 1967], p. 2).

9. A. H. Birch, *Representative and Responsible Government* (London: George Allen and Unwin, 1964), p. 21.

10. This position, often called idealism, is discussed by Birch, *Representation*, and Schubert, *Public Interest*.

is simply to give us what we want."[11] The distinction between wants and needs is sharply drawn by Christian Bay: "Basic human needs are characteristic of the human organism and they are presumably less subject to change than the social or even the physical conditions under which men live. Wants are sometimes manifestations of real needs, but, as Plato and many other wise men since have insisted, we cannot always infer the existence of needs from wants."[12] Needs may emerge and be served through collective discussions led by wise leaders or through the actions of a superior elite, but they are not likely to be the subject of government decision making if left to the independent actions of individual citizens.[13] Thus, another barrier to self-rule is raised.

These potential barriers to popular self-governance—the structural and the individual—are rooted in the assumption that there is a determinable public interest.[14] In the first case it is presumed that this interest is derived through the application of knowledge and/or expertise, in the second through the use of wisdom. In both cases rulers alone, and not ordinary citizens, are presumed to possess a vital quality needed for governance.[15]

11. Joseph Tussman, *Obligation and the Body Politic* (New York: Oxford University Press, 1974), p. 110.
12. Christian Bay, "Politics and Pseudopolitics: A Critical Evaluation of Some Behavioral Literature," *American Political Science Review* 59 (1965): 48.
13. See Birch, *Representation*, pp. 93–95, and Gilbert, "Operative Doctrines," for a summary of the idealist position on the importance of leadership and discussion.
14. For discussions of varying views of the public interest see, among others, Richard E. Flathman, *The Public Interest* (New York: John Wiley and Sons, 1966); Carl J. Friedrich, ed., *Nomos V: The Public Interest* (New York: Atherton Press, 1967); Schubert, *Public Interest*; and Frank J. Sorauf, "The Public Interest Reconsidered," *Journal of Politics* 19 (1967): 616–39.
15. Aberbach, Putnam and Rockman call this the "governance model" on society and public affairs. They contrast it with what they call the "politics model" (Joel D. Aberbach, Robert D. Putnam, and Bert A. Rockman, *Bureaucrats and Politicians in Western Democracies* [Cambridge MA: Harvard University Press, 1981], chap. 5).

Citizen Rule

Other theorists assess the relative abilities of the rulers and the ruled quite differently. They assume that people are highly capable of governing themselves and that the voice (if not the physical presence) of the citizens should be the direct determinant of public policy. One set of thinkers disputes the very concept of a single objective public interest. An array of theorists who share the assumption that interests are multiple and fundamentally subjective, and that the public interest emerges through the interaction of these many interests, are included in this set.[16] These theorists see political decision making as the interplay of many forces, including various private concerns, the technical competence of bureaucrats, and a more general perspective provided by legislators or elected executives. They also consider this interplay to be desirable.

Again, for the purposes of dissecting the problem of bureaucratic control, the substantial differences within this perspective are much less important than the common conception of the abilities of the citizenry. Since there is no separate entity called "the public interest," there is no single group—neither the knowledgeable nor the wise—that has particular capabilities for governing. Ability is presumed to be dispersed widely throughout the polity.

16. The concept of interest as subjective and highly individual is probably most clearly seen in the writings of the utilitarians such as Bentham and the two Mills. For a discussion of the political implications of this idea of interest, see Birch, *Representation*, and Pitkin, *Concept of Representation*. The idea that there are multiple interests in society has been a dominant strain in American political thought, starting with Madison in *The Federalist Papers* (1787–88), further developed by John C. Calhoun in *A Disquisition on Government* (1850; reprint, Indianapolis: Bobbs-Merrill, 1953), and more recently reflected in group theorists such as David B. Truman, *The Governmental Process* (New York: Knopf, 1951). Madison, of course, disputed the desirability of this state of affairs, but argued for a political system carefully constructed around its inevitability.

A second cluster of arguments for popular ability makes a stronger assumption about citizen capacities, while removing the emphasis on the multiplicity of interests. In outline, this position is that of the radical democrat. Perhaps its most well-known variant is what Robert Dahl calls "populist democracy," and an insistence on majority rule is the central tenet.[17] According to this theory, the principles of popular sovereignty and political equality combine to create the fundamental rule that "in choosing among alternatives, the alternative preferred by the greater number is selected."[18] Each citizen, by definition, is presumed to be equally able to determine the course of government action since expressed preferences are the only legitimate basis for such action. Peter Bachrach explains that the democrat "being unable to claim that his values are true for all men and for all time, he is unwilling to impose them upon his fellow men . . . each individual's judgment on the general direction and character of political policies is given weight equal with all others."[19] A more extreme form of radical democracy, derived largely from the thought of Rousseau, stresses the importance of participation.[20] From this perspective democracy requires much more than majority rule. It requires the direct involvement of all citizens in the governmental process.

THE RULERS, THE RULED, AND THE BUREAUCRATS

Modern democratic thought offers us a number of perspectives on the question, How capable are people of gov-

17. Dahl, *Preface to Democratic Theory*, chap. 2.
18. Ibid., pp. 37–38.
19. Bachrach, *Theory of Democratic Elitism*, p. 3.
20. Carole Pateman develops this perspective into what she calls the theory of participatory democracy (Pateman, *Participation and Democratic Theory* [Cambridge: Cambridge University Press, 1970], chap. 2).

erning themselves? The responses range from "not very
capable at all" to "competent by definition." It also offers
us a series of arguments about the nature of politics. Policy questions are variously viewed as technical issues, efforts to fulfill the public interest as divined by a qualified
few, group conflicts, or questions about the will of the
majority (or of the entire populace). The possibilities are
surely more extensive, but these alternatives are sufficient
to explore one of the normative dimensions of our map
of democratic control of bureaucracy. Because these conceptions are derived from the traditional debate about
the relative abilities of the rulers and the ruled, however,
and because that debate does not convert directly to the
bureaucratic variant of the question, we must translate
each alternative into a position on the map.

The Realm of Loose Constraint

The realm of loose constraint is, by definition, a realm of
considerable bureaucratic discretion. It is supported by
the belief that the implementers are significantly more
capable than both the ruled and the elected rulers. Bureaucrats must be allowed a great deal of latitude because
as administrative experts they are uniquely competent to
serve public needs.[21] This conclusion, in turn, is usually
premised on the assumption that there are structural bar-

21. As Joseph A. Schumpeter argues, "Democratic government in modern
industrial society must be able to command . . . the services of a well-trained
bureaucracy. . . . Such a bureaucracy is the main answer to the argument about
government by amateurs. . . . It is not enough that the bureaucracy should be
efficient in current administration and competent to give advice. It must also
be strong enough to guide and, if need be, to instruct the politicians who head
ministries. In order to be able to do this it must be in a position to evolve
principles of its own and sufficiently independent to assert them. It must be a
power in its own right" (Schumpeter, *Capitalism, Socialism and Democracy* [New
York: Harper and Row, 1962], p. 293).

riers to citizen rule. It is the complexity of modern government that places the bureaucrats in their advanta-
geous position.

Complexity, as discussed earlier, has two basic sources:
the scale of government, and the technical difficulty of
public policy issues. Although both are impediments to
citizen rule, the former might not be a hindrance to
elected officials and thus might not translate into a justification for extensive bureaucratic discretion. After all, is
it not the business of elected officials to know their way
around government? To some extent, of course, the answer is yes; but this was much more the case in the days
of simpler and smaller government. Today, government
functions have become so diverse and so extensive that
even full-time representatives find it impossible to keep
track of all that is going on. Over thirty years ago Robert
Dahl and Charles Lindblom argued that the number of
government decisions and the detail, expertise, and speed
involved combine to create a situation in which "the role
of legislative politicians in deliberately shaping the great
bulk of the decisions made by executive politicians is ex-
ceedingly attenuated. They are umpires, who sometimes
rule the ball out of bounds; but they do not carry the ball
themselves or, except by enforcing the basic rules, determine the strategy."[22] The passage of three decades has
only reinforced the pattern.[23] Governmental insiders
have themselves become outsiders when compared to the
bureaucrats involved with the day-to-day administration

22. Robert A. Dahl and Charles E. Lindblom, *Politics, Economics and Welfare*
(1953; reprint, Chicago: University of Chicago Press, 1976), p. 321.
    23. Robert A. Dahl recently wrote: "In modern democratic countries the
complexity of the patterns, processes and activities of a large number of relatively autonomous organizations has outstripped theory, existing information,
the capacity of the system to transmit such information as exists, and the ability
of representatives—or others, for that matter—to comprehend it" (Dahl, *Dilemmas of Pluralist Democracy* [New Haven: Yale University Press, 1982], p. 52).

of programs. As Lippmann wrote, "Only the insider can make decisions, not because he is inherently a better man but because he is so placed that he can understand and act."[24]

If a focus on the sheer scale of government translates into an argument for relatively unconstrained bureaucratic behavior, an emphasis on the technical component of government policies does so even more strongly. While elected leaders may be more capable of mastering technical complexity than ordinary citizens, either because they constitute a superior elite or because they have more time and resources to devote to studying the issues, their limits are also likely to be reached quickly. Indeed, virtually by definition, the more political issues are seen to encompass technical questions, the greater the necessity for discretion by the technical experts—that is, the bureaucrats. In what has probably become the classic statement of this position, Friedrich argues that "throughout the length and breadth of our technical civilization there is arising a type of responsibility on the part of the permanent administrator, the man who is called upon to seek and find the creative solutions for our crying technical needs, which cannot effectively be enforced except by fellow technicians who are capable of judging his policy in terms of the scientific knowledge bearing upon it."[25]

Both kinds of governmental complexity, then, limit not only the ability of citizens but also the ability of their elected leaders to govern; both argue for the necessity of bureaucratic discretion. Thus one normative foundation for relatively loose forms of control of bureaucracy is the belief that political decisions involve highly specialized

24. Lippmann, *Essential Lippmann*, p. 114.
25. Carl J. Friedrich, "Public Policy and the Nature of Administrative Responsibility," in Carl Friedrich and Edward Mason, eds., *Public Policy, 1940* (Cambridge MA: Harvard University Press, 1940), p. 14.

and/or technical issues. Consequently, the best government is government by experts.

The Realm of Tight Constraint

The other major set of impediments to citizen rule—the alleged inability of most individuals to perceive either their own or collective needs—might appear also to support the need for bureaucratic discretion. However, unlike the argument that citizens are not expert enough to discern public needs, the position that they are not wise enough does not necessarily translate into an argument for the superiority of bureaucrats at governance. If leadership, leisure, and distance from the daily wants of the populace are the requisites for effective and responsible decision making, then elected leaders should be favorably equipped. One of the great virtues of representative government is supposed to be that the leaders will possess these qualities and are therefore in a favorable position to serve the public interest.[26] Although a flawed political sense may be an impediment to the ability of ordinary citizens alone to rule, it is not an argument for the comparative advantage of bureaucrats over elected leaders, and hence is not an argument for bureaucratic discretion.

In fact, the contrary is true. From this perspective the narrow, specialized view of the bureaucrat is a liability, not a virtue. If determining the public interest is the task of the wise leaders of the community, then the bureaucrats must be highly subservient and closely follow their directives. Instead of implying relatively weak forms of control as structural barriers do, individual barriers derived from

26. See, for example, *The Federalist Papers* (1787–88; reprint, New York: Mentor Books, 1961), especially numbers 10, 57, 62, and 63.

the belief that ordinary people do not know the public interest imply the need for much tighter forms of constraint by wise leaders.

Some scholars have proposed a hybrid perspective, agreeing that the public interest is determinable only by the wise few, but suggesting that these few include bureaucrats. Thus, they use a public-interest perspective to justify bureaucratic discretion, not bureaucratic constraint. Merle Fainsod, for example, argues that administrators "are capable of recognizing some interests as more 'public' or more 'general' than other interests and of adapting, fusing and directing group pressures toward such a recognition."[27] Glendon Schubert, in discussing what he calls the idealist position that the public is "an incompetent source of public policy," argues that "idealists would maximize (or, at the very least, expand) the scope of official autonomy and discretion," including that of bureaucrats.[28]

The hybrid position, however, is somewhat problematic. Its proponents rarely give reasons for supposing that bureaucrats are any more capable than the disqualified citizenry. Moreover, grouping elected officials and appointed administrators together creates an analytic tangle, since the discretion of each cannot be maximized simultaneously. Unless one believes that expertise allows bureaucrats to transcend narrow private wants,[29] the prior assumptions about the nature of the public interest favor the discretion of elected leaders, and hence limit that of bureaucrats. Furthermore, the belief that expertise carries with it greater vision shifts the terms of debate

27. Merle Fainsod, "Some Reflections on the Nature of the Regulatory Process," in Friedrich and Mason, eds., *Public Policy*, p. 320.
28. Schubert, *Public Interest*, pp. 79, 80.
29. Emmette Redford in fact takes this position in "The Protection of the Public Interest with Special Reference to Administrative Regulation," *American Political Science Review* 48 (1954): 1103–13.

away from the need for wisdom and toward our first set of arguments against citizen ability, the need for specialized expertise. Despite these inconsistencies, the justification for administrative discretion based on superior bureaucratic wisdom becomes an important one empirically. As we shall see in chapter 4, it is often used by the bureaucrats themselves.

A quite different perspective on citizen ability, namely, radical democracy, shares the realm of tight constraint with the public-interest perspective. To radical democrats all citizens are completely capable of governing, and there are therefore no liabilities in very close control of bureaucracy. From this viewpoint the job of bureaucrats is to do exactly as the people, or as their chosen representatives, say.[30] Herman Finer writes, "I again insist upon subservience, for I still am of the belief with Rousseau that the people can be unwise but cannot be wrong. . . . the servants of the public are not to decide their own course; they are to be responsible to the elected representatives of the public, and these are to determine the course of action of the public servants to the most minute degree that is technically feasible."[31] Here, then, good government comes not from the expert, not from the wise, but directly from the will of the people themselves. There is only one relevant competence, and that is vox populi.

The Realm of Moderate Constraint

We have just seen that quite different normative assumptions about the nature of political interest and about the

---

30. Schubert calls this "rationalism." As he describes it, "It is in the public interest . . . to rationalize governmental decision-making processes so that they will automatically result in the carrying out of the Public Will. Human discretion is minimized or eliminated by defining it out of the decision-making situation; responsibility lies in automatic behavior" (Schubert, *Public Interest*, p. 31).

31. Herman Finer, "Administrative Responsibility in Democratic Government," *Public Administration Review* 1 (1941): 339, 336.

abilities of citizens and of their leaders are embedded in the areas of loose and of tight constraint. But what of the region where democratic control of bureaucracy allows for a moderate amount of bureaucratic discretion? In that realm the underlying assumptions are that political interests are multiple and subjective, that there are many relevant competences for governing, and that ability to rule is fairly evenly distributed. These beliefs translate into the belief that competence is shared among the rulers, the ruled, and the bureaucrats. Taken alone, the assumption that all citizens are capable of serving their own interests arguably translates into a proposal that citizens should tightly control the actions of bureaucrats. However, the companion assumption, that many different legitimate interests exist in society and that no single one constitutes the public interest, provides the key to the implications for bureaucratic control of this perspective. If all are qualified to rule, if interests are varied, and if no one interest is objectively superior, then there is little justification for the concentration of power in any single place, since no one group can lay claim to a particular ability to govern.[32] Instead, on the basis of these beliefs, power should be dispersed so that many interests may be represented and no one alone will dominate.[33]

A moderately constrained bureaucracy holds several virtues from this perspective. To the extent that citizens or their representatives do limit bureaucratic discretion, the belief that citizens are capable of governing is reaffirmed. But since dispersion of authority is a crucial way

32. As Robert A. Dahl has argued, one of the primary conditions for procedural democracy (the form of democracy he advocates) is that "no members of the association are in any relevant characteristic so clearly more qualified as to justify their making decisions for all the others" (Dahl, "On Removing Certain Impediments to Democracy in the United States," *Political Science Quarterly* 92 [1977]: 11).

33. See *The Federalist Papers*, numbers 10 and 51.

of accommodating multiple interests, too much constraint from any one source is a problem. The bureaucracy thus joins the legislature as an arena in which contending interests compete.[34] Moderating constraint
allows diverse interests to be heard and allows the latitude
of action that is vital if compromises among interests are
to be reached.[35]

Regions of the Map

Four perspectives on citizen ability have now been translated into a viewpoint on the proper degree of bureaucratic discretion, and each may thus now be located on
the map. I will call these perspectives government according to experts, government according to the public interest determined by wise leaders, government according to
the public interest determined by the people, and government according to the interplay of many interests and
groups. If the map is interpreted as a set of concentric
bands starting at the lower left-hand corner, with the farthest band signifying the greatest constraint, then our

34. Douglas Yates calls this the pluralist logic for bureaucracy (Yates, *Bureaucratic Democracy* [Cambridge MA: Harvard University Press, 1982], chap.
1). Aberbach, Putnam, and Rockman call it the politics model (*Bureaucrats and
Politicians*, pp. 141–42). Stephen H. Linder similarly finds a rationale for discretion and bargaining in bureaucracies in pluralist thought (Linder, "Administrative Accountability: Administrative Discretion, Accountability, and External Controls," in Scott Greer, Ronald Hedlund, and James L. Gibson, eds.,
Accountability in Urban Society: Public Agencies Under Fire [Beverly Hills CA: Sage
Publications, 1978], pp. 181–96. Vincent Ostrom's model of democratic administration is also premised on dispersion of authority (Ostrom, *The Intellectual
Crisis in American Public Administration* [University AL: University of Alabama
Press, 1974]), chap. 4.
35. Dahl and Lindblom, for example, contend that "no one should suppose
that by administrative fiat they can possibly overcome the fundamental lack of
coordination inherent in the American political process; and to any person who
believes polyarchy is desirable, the solution should be a repugnant one even if
it were possible" (*Politics, Economics and Welfare*, p. 351).

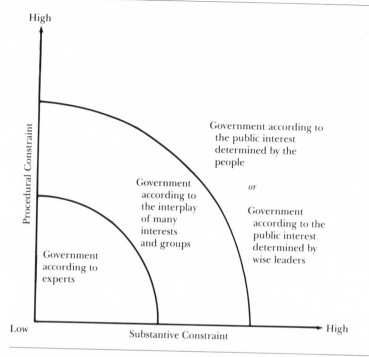

Figure 3. Public Ability and Bureaucratic Constraint

four perspectives take their places as shown in Figure 3. As with most terrains, the topography of democratic control of bureaucracy is not marked by abrupt changes in geology. The bands are not intended to demarcate radical shifts in discretion but rather gradual shadings. Similarly, assumptions about citizen abilities blend at the fringes. Thus, while graphically the bands appear as sharp borders, they are not intended to signify such.[36]

36. I have described and located what may be thought of as pure positions on the map. Many, of course, may take somewhat less pure stands and think competence varies depending upon the circumstances involved. Some, for example, may think citizens are more competent to judge substantive ends than

The bands do, however, represent substantially different normative regions. For those who see the people as competent, the critical question is whether this competence lies in their collective capacity or in the results of their individual and group pursuits of their own wants. If the former, then the outermost band is occupied; if the latter, the central one. For those who do not see the people as competent, the issue becomes how well their elected representatives can fulfill the function of serving the people's interests.[37] The innermost band reflects the position that they cannot; the outermost stands on the assumption that they can very well. In the center, representatives are presumed to be one of many able participants in government decision making.

Who Constrains?

There remains, however, a seeming anomaly. Two quite different sets of assumptions support the farthest band: the belief that people are intrinsically incapable of serving their own interests (and must therefore be governed by wise leaders) and the belief that they are supremely capable of ruling themselves. Each belief supports tight constraint of bureaucrats, but they differ dramatically over who is capable of imposing constraint. The anomaly arises from the translation of the original question about the relative capabilities of the rulers and the ruled to a bureaucratic variant. In order to do this I considered the

---

procedural issues, or vice versa. These people would alter their preferred location on the map according to the particulars of the circumstances they were considering. I discuss a major source of variation in competence—differences among policy areas—in chapter 5.

37. I take here Pitkin's definition of representation as "acting for" the interests of the constituents (*Concept of Representation*, chap. 6).

people and their representatives jointly and then analyzed various perspectives on their abilities compared to
those of bureaucrats. These two perspectives nestled together in the outer band share the belief that the citizen-
representative combination is highly competent, but they
diverge over whether this competence lies with the citizens or with their leaders.

As this anomaly suggests, there is a third issue surrounding democratic control of bureaucracy that is not
directly represented in our map. Control mechanisms not
only constrain bureaucratic behavior to different extents,
and constrain different aspects of behavior, they are also
imposed by different political actors. Any position on the
map implies a given degree of constraint on bureaucratic
discretion, but this constraint may variously be exerted by
individual citizens, organized groups of citizens, legislators, or elected executives. Strategies for control involving
comparable limits on bureaucratic discretion but entail-
ing intervention by different actors may thus occupy the
same band on the map. The extent of constraint is premised on how much competence the citizens and their representatives are presumed to have relative to the bureaucrats, but the choice of an actor to exercise the control
rests on beliefs about who has this competence.

DEMOCRATIC GOVERNMENT: FREEDOM
FROM OPPRESSION OR SELF-RULE?

Should control be exerted over the procedures bureaucrats use to make decisions or over the substance of their
actions? The issues surrounding citizen competence tell
us little about this question and therefore constitute only
one normative dimension of our map of bureaucratic

control. To explore the normative component of choice between procedural and substantive constraint, we must turn to another issue: the role of democratic government. As with the problem of citizen competence, I start with a traditional question and then translate it into a bureaucratic variant. I begin with two fundamental conceptions of democratic government: first, that the distinguishing characteristic of such governments is that they secure and preserve the liberties of the citizens; second, that the essence of a democracy lies in the fact that public power is used to serve collective ends. Theorists have expressed this duality in many ways. Isaiah Berlin writes of two concepts of freedom, a negative freedom from interference or coercion by others and a positive freedom to be part of the group doing the interfering.[38] George Sabine discusses two strands of democratic thought, one emphasizing liberty, the other equality.[39] Both Berlin and Sabine trace the origins of the dualism to the philosophies guiding the English and French Revolutions respectively. In the American context, Dahl writes of two goals for democracy: the Madisonian quest for a nontyrannical republic and the desire for popular sovereignty.[40] Although there are important differences among these pairs of concepts, they each make the essential distinction between popular control as a means of preventing governmental oppression and popular control as a means of harnessing governmental power to public purposes.

At the heart of the first, or liberty-seeking, perspective on democratic government are the idea of a bounded

38. Isaiah Berlin, *Two Concepts of Liberty* (Oxford: Clarendon Press, 1958), pp. 6–19.
39. George H. Sabine, "The Two Democratic Traditions," *Philosophical Review* 61 (1952): 451–74.
40. Dahl, *Preface to Democratic Theory*, pp. 34–36.

state and the goal of preserving it. Berlin argues: "I am normally said to be free to the degree to which no human being interferes with my activity. Political liberty in this sense is simply the area within which a man can do what he wants. . . . It follows that a frontier must be drawn between the area of private life and that of public authority . . . liberty in this sense means liberty from; absence of interference beyond the shifting, but always recognizable, frontier."[41] From this perspective there is a legitimate range of government activity, but there is also a realm government must not enter. A primary function of democratic government is to honor and protect this second realm.[42]

Historically, this tradition is rooted in Madisonian and English liberal thought. In the nineteenth century it was taken to an extreme by John C. Calhoun in his theory of concurrent majorities. Calhoun argued that governments naturally tend toward oppression since they are composed of men, and men naturally seek to exalt their own private interests. The only way to prevent the consequent oppression is to give all interests in society a veto over all government actions that affect them. This is the system of concurrent majorities. He goes on to argue that it is "this negative power—the power of preventing or arresting the action of the government . . . which in fact forms the constitution."[43]

In sharp contrast is the idea of a powerful state that is central to the second, or action-seeking, concept of de-

41. Berlin, *Two Concepts of Liberty*, pp. 7, 9, 11.
42. As Douglas W. Rae points out, in so doing the public power of government is being used to preserve a private status quo, surely an active goal (Rae, "The Limits of Consensual Decision, *American Political Science Review* 69 [1975]: 1289–94. Nonetheless, I will persist in calling this the liberty-seeking perspective.
43. Calhoun, *Disquisition on Government*, p. 28.

mocracy. In this case, political equality is seen as consisting not of equal rights and freedoms but of an equal share in governmental decision making. A democratic government exists in order to take actions to serve the interests of its citizens. Freedom lies in the ability of each of the citizens to shape what those actions will be.[44] In the extreme case Rousseau argues that there is no private realm to be protected by the state; there are no forbidden areas of activity: "Each of us places in common his person and all of his power under the supreme direction of the general will; and as one body we all receive each member as an indivisible part of the whole."[45]

Two kinds of theories fall within this general perspective: those emphasizing specific ends the state should seek and those focusing on processes that ensure that citizen preferences determine government policy, most notably majority rule. The first category includes both the radical arguments that democratic government should act to achieve either socioeconomic equality[46] or psychological fulfillment[47] for its citizens and the generally conservative calls for democratic government to secure social stability or economic progress.[48] Prominent within the second category is the tradition of American populism[49] (which has

44. Berlin describes this "positive" sense of freedom. "I am free if, and only if, I plan my life in accordance with my own will; plans entail rules; a rule does not oppress me or enslave me if I impose it on myself consciously, or accept it freely . . . the notion of liberty . . . is not the 'negative' conception of a field without obstacles, a vacuum in which I can do as I please, but the notion of self-direction or self-control" (*Two Concepts of Liberty*, pp. 28–29).
45. Jean-Jacques Rousseau, *The Social Contract* (New York: Hafner, 1947), p. 15.
46. This perspective is described in Robert D. Putnam, *The Beliefs of Politicians* (New Haven: Yale University Press, 1973), p. 163.
47. See, for example, Bay, "Politics and Pseudopolitics."
48. Giovanni Sartori, *Democratic Theory* (New York: Praeger, 1965), pp. 103–5.
49. See Dahl, *Preface to Democratic Theory*, chap. 2.

championed both decidedly progressive and strikingly regressive causes). All share a conception of democratic government as a positive force acting to achieve certain goals.

Translating these two perspectives to the problem of bureaucracy is a reasonably straightforward procedure. The traditional question considers the relationship between the citizens and the government and asks why citizens seek to control their leaders. The translation again consists of combining the citizens and their elected representatives and of then asking why this combined group (or any part of it) seeks to control bureaucracy. The first, or liberty-seeking, perspective on democracy answers, In order to prevent the abuse of power. The second, or action-seeking, perspective replies, To secure the proper use of power. These two alternatives, in turn, support the procedural and substantive axes of the map of bureaucratic control as shown in Figure 4.

If democracy means a government that respects individual rights, and if, therefore, control over bureaucracy is sought in order to prevent a violation of these rights, then the relevant control is constraint over bureaucratic procedures. That is because the central concern of people who share this perspective is not what the state should do but what the state should *not* do. One way of ensuring that the state does not violate liberty is to require that bureaucrats follow specified procedural norms.[50] The norms may be couched in terms of what the bureaucrats must do—for example, that they must consult certain

50. Writing about red tape, surely one of the most lamented procedural constraints, Herbert Kaufman finds its origins in a concern for liberty: "A society less concerned about the rights of individuals in government and out might well be governed with a much smaller volume of paper and much simpler and faster administrative procedures than are typical of governance in this country" (Kaufman, *Red Tape* [Washington DC: Brookings Institution, 1977], p. 46).

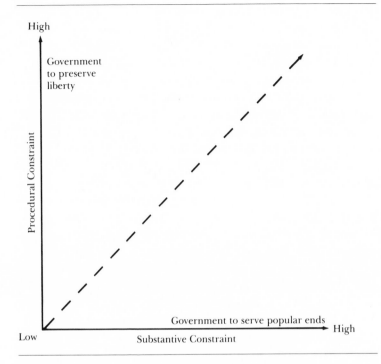

Figure 4. Democratic Government and the Nature of Constraint

groups; but this is a way of ensuring that they do *not* act counter to certain interests or do *not* violate certain rights.[51]

If, on the other hand, democracy consists of citizens sharing in government decision making, and if, therefore, control over bureaucracy is sought in order to ensure that bureaucratic power is used to further the ends

51. Once again, parallels to theories of representation arise. This distinction is similar to the one Pitkin makes between representation as acting for—i.e., as a concept referring to the nature of the representative's decisions—and other more formal theories. See Pitkin, *Concept of Representation*, pp. 112–15.

the citizens have decided upon, then the relevant control is constraint of the substance of bureaucratic decisions. By constraining substance one ensures that bureaucrats work to achieve the ends set by the citizens. Still unanswered is whether these two goals for democratic government are compatible. Figure 4 implies that the goals can coexist and that all possible mixtures may be achieved. Along each axis, one goal dominates. As one moves toward the diagonal, the mix includes increasing proportions of the other until the diagonal where both goals are equally sought. My intent is not to argue for perfect compatibility, however, but rather merely to allow for that possibility. Virtually all answers to the question of compatibility have been proposed at some time.[52] If one believes that popular control to preserve liberty and popular control to ensure the proper use of state power cannot coexist, then only positions on the map along the two axes are conceivable. If one believes that both these goals may be realized in some measure, then additional locations moving toward the diagonal enter into the realm of logical consistency; and if one believes they are totally compatible, then all positions on the map are possible. What one considers possible is not, of course, necessarily the same as what one considers desirable. Preferences determine where one actually chooses to go, but logical possibilities limit the range of choice.[53]

    52. See, for example, Berlin, *Two Concepts of Liberty*, pp. 14–16, for the position that negative and positive freedom are irreconcilable; Tussman, *Body Politic*, pp. 25–30, for the argument that liberty is granted in return for the granting of state power; and Sabine, "Two Democratic Traditions," pp. 465–74, for a statement of their interdependence.
    53. The question of whether all positions on the map are, in fact, conceivable also arises. If all combinations of answers to the two sets of normative issues are not possible—i.e., if ability and goals are inherently linked—then certain areas of the map cannot logically exist. For example, if a liberty-seeking perspective was always joined to the belief that there are multiple, subjective interests in society, then the areas to the left (or liberty-seeking side) of the diagonal would be limited to the space defined by the central band.

NORMATIVE BELIEFS
AND POLITICAL REALITY

When people argue about mechanisms for controlling bureaucracy, they generally focus on practical details. As we have just seen, however, fundamental normative questions concerning popular ability and the role of democratic government lie beneath the specific differences among control mechanisms. Often conflict over specifics masks debate over basic beliefs.

Controversies about clientele-oriented strategies of control lying in the central area of the map (Fig. 2) are a clear example. These strategies involve strengthening the ties between various societal groups and administrative agencies. Specific devices include advisory boards and formal group representation within an agency, and as Herbert Kaufman writes, "These practices are often assailed for giving too much weight to special interests as against the public interest, and their efficacy in furthering the cause of justice and rationality has been sharply questioned."[54] A focus on the efficacy of such strategies may be misplaced, however, since frequently what separates opponents from proponents is not a difference of opinion about how well a particular advisory mechanism works, but disagreements about whether group interests are "special" interests and hence any different from the public interest. Strategies lying in the central band of the map (Fig. 3) are premised on the assumption that group interests are not "special" interests, whereas critics of these strategies think they are.[55] Thus, controversy over an ad-

54. Kaufman, *Red Tape*, p. 48.
55. Grant McConnell, for example, sharply attacks group-based political institutions: "Far from providing guarantees of liberty, equality, and concern for the public interest, organization of political life by small constituencies tends to enforce conformity, to discriminate in favor of elites, and to eliminate public values from effective political consideration" (McConnell, *Private Power and American Democracy* [New York: Random House, Vintage Books, 1970], p. 6).

visory board may, in fact, reflect disagreement over the nature of interest in society. A focus on the narrow instrumental question will not resolve the underlying dispute.

Normative issues virtually by definition involve questions of belief, but this does not mean that they are completely immune to empirical evaluation. Some policy arguments are rooted in irreconcilable differences of basic belief, but other debates over control strategies are produced by a discrepancy between normative assumptions and the actual political context in which control takes place. Just as economic actors are not always the rational beings some economic theory presumes, political actors often defy normative expectations. A control mechanism premised on assumptions about political behavior that are not fulfilled is likely to be a control mechanism that does not work according to plan.

One way political reality may intrude lies in the roles political actors actually choose. A vivid example is found among control strategies lying in the outer band of our map (Fig. 3) that involve the imposition of constraint by legislators. Such proposals are premised on the assumption that there is a public interest that can be achieved through enlightened leaders who transcend the narrow focus of ordinary citizens.[56] If legislators behave little differently than the people who elect them, however, the expected enlightened intervention will not occur, and the intended control in the interest of broader public values will fail. Recent studies of the U.S. Congress indicate that this is often precisely the case. David Mayhew, for example, argues that the incentives facing members of Congress impel them to display

56. Theodore J. Lowi's call for juridical democracy in *The End of Liberalism* (New York: Norton, 1969) is perhaps the best, but by no means the only, example.

a strong tendency to wrap policies in packages that are salable as particularized benefits . . . they tend in framing laws to give a particularistic cast to matters that do not obviously require it. . . . The quest for the particular impels Congressmen to take a vigorous interest in the organization of the federal bureaucracy. Thus, for example, the Corps of Army Engineers, structured to undertake discrete district projects, must be guarded from presidents who will submerge it in a quest for planning.[57]

To the extent that Mayhew is right that members of Congress have an incentive to pursue particularistic interests, no amount of tinkering with congressional control over the bureaucracy will produce coordinated control in the "public interest," and strategies based on that assumption are doomed to fail.[58] Worse still is the possibility that elected officials will attempt to control bureaucracies for the primary purpose of self-enrichment or self-aggrandizement. In that case control will serve neither the public interest nor the interests of ordinary citizens but only the individual interests of elected officials.

Control strategies based on the assumption that citizens or their representatives have sufficient expertise to control bureaucrats may also be vulnerable to undesired mutation if the assumption proves to be unfounded empirically. Dahl emphasizes the importance of what he calls "enlightened understanding" to democracy. "For if people regularly choose means that impede rather than facilitate attaining their goals, or if they invariably choose

---

57. David R. Mayhew, *Congress: The Electoral Connection* (New Haven: Yale University Press, 1974), pp. 127, 128, 131. Arthur Maass, in *Muddy Waters* (Cambridge MA: Harvard University Press, 1951), and Lewis C. Mainzer in *Political Bureaucracy* (Glenview IL: Scott, Foresman, 1973) make similar arguments about congressional behavior vis-à-vis the bureaucracy.
58. There is also evidence that executive branch control will produce similar results. See, for example, Dahl and Lindblom, *Politics, Economics and Welfare*, pp. 342, 352.

goals that damage their deeper needs, then of how much value is the process?" he asks.[59] Jerry Mashaw makes the point concretely in the context of a specific agency, the Social Security Administration. He is skeptical about increased claimant involvement as a way of controlling the bureaucracy, because claimants cannot command the information necessary to make involvement effective. "Without understanding, participation or control becomes an obvious and cruel joke rather than an assurance of fairness."[60]

A second way political reality may clash with democratic belief is if only some actors perform their expected roles. Control strategies premised on the assumption that government should serve the preference of the majority will not perform as expected when the majority do not express preferences at all.[61] If most people do not have preferences on most issues, control mechanisms based on the assumption that they do may actually work to serve the interests not of the majority but of a self-selected mi-

59. Dahl, "On Removing Certain Impediments to Democracy," p. 18. Holden maintains that "the idea that 'higher authority' alone could either know enough of all the relevant situations or afford to make continuous readjustments of agency missions simply ignores the complex reality" (Matthew Holden, Jr., "Imperialism in Bureaucracy," *American Political Science Review* 60 [1966]: 950). Birch makes a similar point about legislative-administrative relations in British government in *Representative and Responsible Government*, pp. 150–53.

60. Jerry Mashaw, *Bureaucratic Justice* (New Haven: Yale University Press, 1983), p. 141.

61. In a study in depth of political ideology, Robert E. Lane, for example, found that the expression of political grievances was unusual among the men he spoke with (Lane, *Political Ideology* [New York: Free Press, 1962], p. 455). Philip E. Converse reviews the evidence on the nature of political information and voting in his "Public Opinion and Voting Behavior," in Fred L. Greenstein and Nelson W. Polsby, eds., *Handbook of Political Science*, vol. 4 (Reading MA: Addison-Wesley Publishing Co., 1975), as do Donald R. Kinder and David O. Sears in their "Public Opinion and Political Action," in Gardner Lindzey and Elliot Aronson, eds., *Handbook of Social Psychology*, 3d ed. (New York: Random House, 1985).

nority. Once again, debates over minor modification in such strategies may miss a fundamental issue.

Selective action can also plague control strategies that assume that the public interest is served through the interaction of multiple interests in society. Even if one accepts this assumption, control strategies based on it may suffer if in reality only a subset of all interests are represented in the interaction. Typically this subset might consist of organized groups and actors who are in other ways powerful.[62] In this case, too, problems raised by specific strategies may not lie within the narrow architecture of the means of control, but rather in the broader context in which the control functions. Economic and political inequality may work to impede some groups from expressing their interests. When this is true the necessary conditions for the achievement of the public interest will be absent, even if the basic theory is sound.[63] Alternatively, the incentives built into the structure of political organizations may encourage them to pursue some interests but not others.[64] In that case as well, only some interests will be expressed and control strategies premised on the assumption that all interests are expressed will be undercut.

We have now seen that different control strategies rely on

62. Many critics have noted that group-based control strategies tend to be dominated by the already organized. See, among others, Louis L. Jaffe, "The Effective Limits of the Administrative Process," in Alan Altshuler, ed., *The Politics of the Federal Bureaucracy* (New York: Dodd, Mead, 1968); Avery Leiserson, *Administrative Regulation* (Chicago: University of Chicago Press, 1942); Lowi, *End of Liberalism*; and Philip Selznick, *TVA and the Grass Roots* (New York: Harper and Row, 1966).

63. Dahl discusses the need for greater economic equality, or at least for ways to prevent economic resources from being converted into political ones if democracy is to function properly ("On Removing Certain Impediments to Democracy," pp. 15–16).

64. Dahl puts forward this argument in *Dilemmas of Pluralist Democracy*, chap. 3.

different assumptions about the goals and methods of democratic government. Understanding the differences among assumptions helps us to understand why people differ in their choices of control strategy and provides a basis for making those choices. Understanding the assumptions also helps to identify cases in which the assumptions are likely to be violated when control strategies are employed in practice. Finally, this analysis begins the assessment of the benefits and costs of using any particular means to control bureaucratic discretion. This assessment will be continued in the next chapter, where I focus on the costs of control.

3

THE COSTS OF CONTROL

From the perspective of the democrat, bringing bureaucratic power under the control of the citizenry is highly desirable. Doing so resolves the contradiction between a political system designed to be under the control of its citizens and a force that seemingly eludes such control. Regardless of the ends one thinks democratic government should achieve and of how one chooses to allocate power among various political actors, controlling bureaucracy should improve the democratic quality of government.

But controlling bureaucracies is not an unmitigated good, and controllers must be aware of the costs as well as the benefits of limiting bureaucratic discretion. Controllers, in fact, face potential costs both when the constraints they place on bureaucratic behavior are observed and when they are not. When constraints are followed, but impair the ability of bureaucrats to achieve public ends, effectiveness costs arise. When constraints are not followed, and controllers are faced with the unhappy choice of committing extensive resources to find out why, or of punishing bureaucrats for failures that may have been beyond their control, enforcement costs arise.[1]

1. Francis E. Rourke's two criteria for judging bureaucracies, responsiveness and effectiveness, in some ways parallel these two costs (Rourke, *Bureaucracy, Politics and Public Policy* [Boston: Little, Brown, 1969], p. 3).

In this chapter I explore these costs of control. I first discuss both costs and examine the circumstances under which each is likely to occur. I then show how control mechanisms lying in different regions of the map developed in chapter 1 are particularly likely to incur effectiveness and/or enforcement costs. Finally, I discuss two complications that further increase the likelihood that controlling bureaucracies will incur these costs.

EFFECTIVENESS AND ENFORCEMENT

Effectiveness Costs

Effectiveness costs occur when controllers constrain a bureaucrat in ways that undermine the bureaucrat's ability to do his or her job.[2] Since effectiveness is supposedly one of the primary virtues of bureaucracy,[3] this cost may be a serious one indeed.[4]

Effectiveness costs are created in one of two ways: (1) Controllers may tell bureaucrats to do the wrong thing— that is, to behave in a way that will not achieve the goals

2. Guy Benveniste discusses the way control can reduce service quality (Benveniste, *Bureaucracy*, 2d ed. [San Francisco: Boyd and Fraser, 1983], chap. 2).

3. Robert K. Merton, for example, writes, "The chief merit of bureaucracy is its technical efficiency, with a premium placed on precision, speed, expert control, continuity, discretion, and optimal returns on input" (Merton, *Social Theory and Social Structure* [Glencoe IL: Free Press, 1957], p. 196).

4. Robert D. Putnam argues that internal administrative efficiency is an important component of governmental responsiveness (Putnam, "The Political Attitudes of Senior Civil Servants in Western Europe: A Preliminary Report," *British Journal of Political Science* 3 [1973]: 259). Giovanni Sartori, discussing "responsibility" in general, maintains that it has two components: obligation and meeting of given standards (Sartori, "Representational Systems," in David L. Sills, ed., *International Encyclopedia of the Social Sciences*, vol. 13 [New York: Macmillan and Free Press, 1968], p. 468).

that the controllers themselves desire. This would occur if a school board directed all elementary school principals to begin mathematics instruction with calculus. Such a command reflects a fundamental misunderstanding of the progression of skills necessary for learning mathematics. The example is extreme, but many educators can recount stories of what they see as similarly mistaken commands from their school boards. (2) Controllers may impose constraints that are unduly restrictive, preventing bureaucrats from doing their jobs successfully. In this case the problem does not stem from wrong-headed substantive direction, but from the inappropriateness of *any* tight specification of bureaucratic behavior, regardless of its content.[5] Thus mathematics learning might be impaired if a school board ordered principals to devote equal amounts of time to every unit of a math program regardless of how quickly the children learn. Successful mathematics teaching simply requires more flexibility on the part of individual teachers than such a constraint would allow.

Enforcement Costs

Enforcement costs are somewhat more complex. They start with the fact that merely telling a bureaucrat to behave in a certain way does not guarantee compliance. Bureaucrats have many interests besides those of their controllers, and they possess the capacity to pursue them. If they did not, controlling bureaucracies would not be the

---

5. Martin Landau and Russell Stout, Jr., forcefully argue that excessively tight control can limit discretion to the point that effective problem solving is impaired (Landau and Stout, "To Manage is Not to Control: Or the Folly of Type Two Errors," *Public Administration Review* 39 [1979]: 153).

persistent problem it is.[6] To ensure compliance, some monitoring must occur. This need to monitor is itself a cost, of course, since it requires the expenditure of time and money. The cost grows when bureaucrats fail to perform as controllers direct and the latter are faced with the question of whether to impose sanctions. If it is clear that a bureaucrat has deliberately ignored constraints, the decision may be easy. But if it is not clear, the controller is faced with a choice between ignoring violations, and in the process weakening control, or punishing bureaucrats for failing to do things that were not in their power to do. Either course of action can prove costly.

For those who believe that responsibility and accountability go hand in hand, bureaucrats should be punished only for willful disregard of attempts to control them.[7] However, since democratic controls are not the only constraints that affect bureaucrats, the simple test of comparing bureaucratic behavior with a given constraint is not always adequate for determining whether sanctions

6. The literature documenting the divergence of bureaucratic interests from those of public officials is vast. Two major sets of literature in this area are the implementation literature and the public choice literature. The former analyzes the difficult transition from law into functioning public policy; the latter uses microeconomic concepts to analyze bureaucratic incentives. The implementation literature includes such works as Jeffrey L. Pressman and Aaron Wildavsky, *Implementation* (Berkeley and Los Angeles: University of California Press, 1973), and Eugene Bardach, *The Implementation Game* (Cambridge MA: MIT Press, 1977). The public choice literature includes works such as William A. Niskanen, Jr., *Bureaucracy and Representative Government* (Chicago: Aldine-Atherton, 1971), and Albert Breton and Ronald Wintrobe, *The Logic of Bureaucratic Conduct* (Cambridge: Cambridge University Press, 1982).

7. On this point see, for example, Herbert J. Spiro's argument that, in a democracy, the degree that one is accountable for an action should be balanced by the extent that one is causally responsible for it (Spiro, *Responsibility in Government* [New York: Van Nostrand Reinhold, 1969], p. 18). The argument is also related to the common assertion that clear lines of responsibility are necessary for accountability. See Peter M. Blau, *The Dynamics of Bureaucracy*, rev. ed. (Chicago: University of Chicago Press, 1963), p. 142.

should be invoked. To be sure, it seems fair to demand that bureaucrats not permit their personal interests to influence their behavior. However, there are a variety of other constraints that are impossible for bureaucrats to ignore, most notably constraints arising from inadequacies in the state of knowledge in the bureaucrat's field (inadequacies that extend beyond individual failings) and the increasingly common constraint of insufficient resources.[8] When bureaucrats fail to behave in ways that accord with a specific constraint because of factors such as these, and not because of a deliberate effort to circumvent the constraint, those who link accountability to responsibility will surely be reluctant to impose sanctions.

Consider the example of a principal who is told by the school board to have all children reading at grade level by the end of the year. In June the children are tested and a significant number of them fall well below the desired level. Should the principal be punished for not following the school board's directive? It depends on why the children did not learn enough. The principal may have refused to develop a comprehensive reading program, and the teachers may therefore have devoted little time to the subject. Alternatively, the principal may not have had adequate funds to develop and implement a

---

8. Herbert Kaufman points out that "even if a subordinate has no doubts about what his superiors would like him to do in a given situation, and even if he would sincerely like to do what he is told to do, he will occasionally find it impossible to comply. Sometimes it is because his workload prevents him from maintaining maximum standards of quality. . . . Sometimes it is because he has not had adequate training or experience. Sometimes it is because the state of the art he practices is not sufficiently advanced" (Kaufman, *Administrative Feedback* [Washington DC: Brookings Institution, 1973], p. 3). Similarly, Jerry Mashaw argues that bureaucratic performance cannot be measured solely against the ideal of instrumental rationality: "Consideration must be given to the limits of instrumental rationality in the context of a particular administrative program" (Mashaw, *Bureaucratic Justice* [New Haven: Yale University Press, 1983], p. 50).

program that would meet the board's demands. It is also possible that *no* program could be developed that would teach all the children at that school to read with the desired competence. Subscribers to the belief that accountability flows from responsibility would only punish the principal in the first case.

How do we know, however, why the principal failed to conform to the constraint? Answering this would be easy if the principal failed to develop any program at all, but if a new reading program was implemented and reading ability still falls below the norm, the question becomes, Did the principal really try to meet the constraint? It would be difficult to know without asking about the principal's intentions. But an enforcement principle that relies on the intentions of an actor is highly subjective and open to great abuse. Because of the difficulty in knowing whether they are warranted, the likely result in this situation is that sanctions will not be employed.[9] The cumulative result of a series of such failures to invoke sanctions is that the potency of control is diminished and future obedience is less likely.[10]

Others might be less hesitant to punish bureaucrats for failings beyond their control. The growing call for teachers to be held accountable for their students' test scores

9. Michael Lipsky argues that one limit on efforts to control "street-level" bureaucrats is that "a critical piece of information is the state of mind of the worker," information which is in the sole possession of the bureaucrat (Lipsky, *Street-Level Bureaucracy* [New York: Russell Sage Foundation, 1980], p. 163).

10. Jerry Mashaw advances a somewhat different argument about the problems of enforcing constraint. His concern is with the Quality Assurance program in the Social Security disability program. He argues that given the demands for discretion in disability decisions, quality assurance reviews may lead merely to second guessing: "To some degree this problem can be solved by limiting the QA analysts' scope of review. An error is assigned only if it is 'clear.'" He goes on to argue that there are in fact very few clear errors and that one result might be that inappropriate decisions will be allowed to stand (Mashaw, *Bureaucratic Justice*, pp. 149–50).

certainly suggests that this is the case. But enforcement of constraint and punishment of bureaucrats for factors beyond their control pose their own costs to the controller. First, the individual bureaucrats involved may become demoralized, and those who can are likely to seek other employment.[11] Since demoralized bureaucrats are not likely to be effective bureaucrats and those who leave may be hard to replace with others who are equally qualified, controllers may be discouraged from imposing future sanctions.[12] Second, the bureaucrats involved are likely to try to resist or circumvent a constraint they think is beyond their ability to meet.[13] Michael Lipsky describes a number of ways in which bureaucrats subvert performance standards that ignore the exigencies of their work. These include distorting their behavior to conform narrowly to the standard (e.g., teachers teaching the test), neglecting other responsibilities, and inauthentically achieving the standard.[14]

Each of these outcomes is costly to the controller. If the controller is discouraged from enforcing control, the reduction of the potency of control described above will occur. If bureaucrats become deceitful, the controller will

11. Barbara Gelb describes just such a situation in the New York City police department when high-ranking police officials were held accountable for corruption at the lower reaches of their command that they knew nothing about (Gelb, "The Hard Code of the Superchiefs," *New York Times Magazine*, October 9, 1983).

12. Michael Lipsky argues that in street-level bureaucracies the dependence of managers on their workers makes the managers reluctant to sanction negative performance for fear of creating even worse consequences for the delivery of services (*Street-Level Bureaucracy*, p. 163).

13. James D. Thompson argues that "when outcomes are beyond the organization's control, assessment in terms of outcomes is resisted" (Thompson, *Organizations in Action* [New York: McGraw-Hill, 1967], p. 92). Eugene Bardach and Robert A. Kagan argue that legalistic regulatory enforcement can spawn an "organized culture of resistance among regulated firms" in *Going by the Book* (Philadelphia: Temple University Press, 1982), p. 114.

14. Lipsky, *Street-Level Bureaucracy*, pp. 166–67.

have to devote greater resources to monitoring their behavior. If bureaucrats become demoralized, distort their
behavior, neglect their responsibilities, or quit, enforcement of constraint will create effectiveness costs for the
agency, and the seeming arbitrariness will reduce the
sanctions' potency as a deterrent.

COSTS AND UNCERTAINTY

Uncertainty about how to bring about desired ends creates both effectiveness and enforcement costs. It also creates a dilemma for controllers, who are at times forced to
increase the risk of creating one cost in order to avoid the
other. Without uncertainty, controllers know precisely
what the bureaucrats need to do, and control should
therefore create few costs to effectiveness. Similarly, controllers can avoid enforcement costs if they are confident
bureaucrats have the means to achieve the ends specified.
Without uncertainty there should be no problem with determining the reason for noncompliance, and neither
should bureaucrats think they are being punished un-
fairly.[15]

Most problems in public policy, however, abound in uncertainty. In the prevention of crime and the maintenance
of economic growth, for example, it is often impossible
even for specialists to specify in advance which policies
will succeed. Other times, the technical complexity of a

15. Breton and Wintrobe also argue for the role of uncertainty in facilitating what they call "inefficient" bureaucratic behavior. They assert that the possibility of "genuine mistakes" and the inevitability of some distortion of information within the bureaucratic context make it possible for deliberate mistakes
and distortion by bureaucrats to go unpunished (*Logic of Bureaucratic Conduct*,
chap. 3).

problem prevents nonspecialists such as citizens or members of Congress from determining how to reach particular goals. In still other cases the task of the agency requires calibrating bureaucratic actions to a client population that is so highly variable that the calibration cannot be specified in advance.[16] In all of these cases, the imposition of control can be costly.

Generally, controllers can avoid enforcement costs if they narrowly focus constraint on the actions bureaucrats take, and not on the outcomes they are meant to achieve. By definition, a bureaucrat's actions are more firmly under his or her control than the effects of those actions. Punishing a bureaucrat for failing to act in a specified way is therefore likely to be easier than punishing that same bureaucrat for failing to attain a specified outcome.

Unfortunately, such a strategy for avoiding enforcement costs often increases the chances that effectiveness costs will arise. Bureaucratic actions are generally of interest only to the extent that they contribute (or fail to contribute) to achieving public goals. The point of telling a school administrator to introduce a given instructional package, for example, is usually not that the package itself is desirable (unless, of course, one is its author or publisher) but rather that it is a way for children to learn a set of skills. If we are certain that the package will teach children those skills, then there is no problem. If we are uncertain, however, narrow restrictions on the administrator's actions will create precisely the circumstances under which effectiveness may be undermined. Thus, for the great majority of problems there is a conflict between creating situations where bureaucrats can effectively

16. Lipsky argues that this is an essential characteristic of street-level bureaucracies (*Street-Level Bureaucracy*, p. 15).

achieve public ends and creating situations where democratic control can be adequately enforced.[17]

COSTS AND MECHANISMS
OF DEMOCRATIC CONTROL

Some mechanisms of democratic control are more likely
to incur costs than others because they are more likely to
involve constraining bureaucrats to do things we are uncertain about how to do. Others are more likely to constrain bureaucrats in ways that make them unable to deal
with the problems caused by uncertainty. These control
mechanisms are clustered in different regions of the map.
It is not impossible for control mechanisms lying in other
regions to incur effectiveness or enforcement costs, it is
just less likely.

First, substantive constraints are more likely to be
plagued by uncertainty since, in general, our knowledge
is poorer about how to achieve substantive ends than it is
for procedural ends. We know less, for example, about
how to provide adequate housing for all (within reason-
able budgetary limits) than we do about how to establish

17. This argument is a variant on the familiar one that there is a trade-off
between democracy and efficiency. See, among others, Henry B. Mayo, *An Introduction to Democratic Theory* (New York: Oxford University Press, 1960), p.
103, on the general point. "Control of government bureaucracies by political
superiors requires a fine balance: too detailed direction of politicians destroys
the area of discretionary judgment indispensable if rational decisions are to be
made about complex technical questions; yet too little direction means a weakening of polyarchy," Robert A. Dahl and Charles E. Lindblom explain (*Politics,
Economics and Welfare* [New York: Harper Torchbooks, 1953], p. 341). That
there is a tension between a democratic political system's desire to control its
bureaucracies and the need for bureaucracies to do their jobs well is likewise
suggested by both Douglas Yates (*Bureaucratic Democracy* [Cambridge MA: Harvard University Press, 1982], p. 154), and Joel D. Aberbach, Robert D. Putnam,
and Bert A. Rockman (*Bureaucrats and Politicians in Western Democracies* [Cam-
bridge MA: Harvard University Press, 1981], p. 255).

accounting procedures open to outside review. Second, tight constraints by definition give bureaucrats less latitude to deal with uncertainty.[18] Since tight constraints limit maneuverability, the likelihood that being constrained will impair bureaucratic effectiveness increases as constraint gets higher. Thus, the further a control mechanism lies from the origin of the map, the more likely it is to incur effectiveness costs.

Since they frequently constrain bureaucratic behavior in areas of uncertainty, mechanisms for control that lie along the substantive axis, whether tight or loose, carry with them the burden of enforcement costs. Substantive control mechanisms that are also tightly constraining are doubly vulnerable. Loose substantive control, on the other hand, is likely to lessen effectiveness costs by allowing bureaucrats many options.

With these conclusions in hand, we can understand some of the weaknesses and criticisms of existing control mechanisms. We can also predict problems likely to arise with proposed reforms by locating their positions on the map.

Several examples illustrate the potential for prediction. Proposals for radical increases in citizen participation fall in the area of the map where constraint is high and thus within the area where we would expect effectiveness costs to arise. The most notable of these proposals have probably been those for community control of education and anti-poverty programs. An important issue in the debate over these proposals was whether community control would allow for effective delivery of education or anti-poverty services. Where implemented they have been se-

---

18. The concept of unreasonableness put forward by Bardach and Kagan (*Going By The Book*, chap. 3) is a regulatory cousin of effectiveness costs. They argue that unreasonableness is more likely to come from tough regulation.

verely criticized for hindering program effectiveness.[19] The problem is not limited to community control. Herbert Kaufman argues that an agency mired in red tape is in fact an agency whose effectiveness is impaired by extensive constraints on its behavior.[20]

Moving toward the lower right-hand corner of the map, where constraint is both high and heavily substantive, we come to an area where we would expect control mechanisms to create both effectiveness and enforcement problems. Political executives, for example, are appointed to ensure that agency decisions conform to the policies of elected executives. An excessive inflow of political appointees, however, may threaten the effectiveness of an agency in achieving public goals. Relative to political appointees, career bureaucrats typically have superior experience and knowledge necessary for the smooth functioning of programs.[21] The effectiveness problem may be circumvented if the political appointees come to understand the agency through the eyes of the career bureaucrats. If they do, they may constrain the latter in ways the bureaucrats are comfortable with. To the extent that this

19. Daniel P. Moynihan, *Maximum Feasible Misunderstanding* (New York: Free Press, 1970), especially chap. 7. More generally, Herbert Kaufman discusses administrative decentralization in terms of the trade-offs among neutral competence, representativeness, and executive leadership (Kaufman, "Administrative Decentralization and Political Power," *Public Administration Review* 29 (1969): 3–14. Some of Douglas T. Yates's conclusions about neighborhood democracy speak indirectly to this point. He found that the most comprehensive programs were generally unable to exert much control because of the great complexity both of administrative structure and of policy problems (Yates, *Neighborhood Democracy* [Lexington MA: D. C. Heath, 1973], especially chaps. 4 and 7).

20. Herbert Kaufman, *Red Tape* (Washington DC: Brookings Institution, 1977). "The proliferation of rules and regulations prescribing the conduct of decision making—which is presumably what one means by red tape—is inherent in bureaucracy. If discretion is to be limited and prescribed, rules and regulations are necessary," Dahl and Lindblom had also recognized much earlier (*Politics, Economics and Welfare*, p. 248).

21. Frederick C. Mosher, *Democracy and the Public Service* (New York: Oxford University Press, 1968), p. 174.

happens, however, the political appointees will be less capable of enforcing the will of the elected executives who sponsored them.[22]

Near the center of the map, where constraint is moderate and has both substantive and procedural components, we are on the fringe of the region where both effectiveness and enforcement difficulties are likely to arise. The clientele-oriented control mechanisms that lie there are subject to less severe forms of both problems. Because advisory boards, for example, mix substantive and procedural constraints, enforcement issues are less salient, but may still plague the substantive aspects of the intended control. It is relatively easy to ensure that a specified group is consulted. It is another matter to invoke sanctions if the expected outcome is not achieved—that is, if client wishes are not obeyed. Although advisory boards are rarely accused of creating acute effectiveness problems, they have been accused of creating some.[23]

COMPLICATIONS: CONNECTING POLICIES
AND CONFLICTING GOALS

Thus far our discussion of the costs of controlling bureaucratic behavior has proceeded from a reasonably sim-

22. Richard F. Fenno, "The Cabinet Member and Departmental Administration", in Alan Altshuler, ed., *The Politics of the Federal Bureaucracy* (New York: Dodd, Mead, 1968). Comparable problems plague close legislative control. Critics warn that Congress cannot tightly control administrative operation without serious loss to program effectiveness. Matthew Holden, Jr., for example, maintains that "the idea that 'higher authority' alone could either know enough of all the relevant situations or afford to make continuous readjustments of agency missions simply ignores the complex reality" (Holden, "Imperialism in Bureaucracy," *American Political Science Review* 60 [1966]: 950).

23. Kaufman, for example, writes that "the methods of interest representation generate more directives and controls, more steps in the forging of government policies, more bargaining before decisions are reached, and more post decision litigation than would otherwise develop" (*Red Tape*, p. 49). This point will be discussed further below.

ple vision of the world of governmental decision making in which a single controller essentially constrains a single bureaucracy. Real world administrative and policy arenas, unfortunately, are significantly more complicated than this. Bureaucracies are neither isolated from one another nor frozen in time. Decisions one bureaucracy makes reverberate to decisions facing other bureaucracies. Decisions made by a bureaucracy at one time have consequences for future decisions. Such connections mean that one set of constraints on a bureaucracy often has effects that ripple throughout the agency and to other bureaucracies.

Furthermore, there is rarely a single political actor seeking to constrain an agency. More typically, many actors either compete for the right to do so or share in the task of constraint. Moreover, these actors are rarely in full agreement about the goals they think the agency should pursue and about how it should be constrained. Each of these complications—connections among issues and conflict among goals—can significantly aggravate the costs of constraint.

Connections among Issues

We have already seen that control mechanisms that tightly constrain bureaucratic behavior may generate effectiveness costs. When a bureaucrat's problems are connected to one another or to those other bureaucrats deal with, effectiveness costs are more likely. Just as bureaucrats with discretion have more flexibility in dealing with uncertainty, so, too, discretion allows for flexibility in dealing with a group of connected issues. Without it, bureaucrats are less able to avoid the unintended consequences of a given constraint. Program effectiveness may therefore be affected by the repercussions of constraints exerted in the context of other, related issues.

The administrators in a hypothetical housing authority

can serve as an example. They are charged by the city council with finding sites on which to build new low-income housing, but are constrained to choose sites with certain attributes and in a specified time. These constraints may in themselves create effectiveness costs for the agency if, for example, the council is wrong about what constitutes an appropriate site, or if the council list does not allow the administrators to balance the assets and liabilities of specific sites. If we add to the picture the fact that the authority is engaged in developing an ambitious tenant management program that is commanding a substantial amount of staff time, we begin to see the complications wrought by connecting policies. By tightly constraining the time period for the site search, the council may force the administrators to conduct neither the search nor the program development effectively. A less tight constraint might allow the administrators better to juggle the competing claims on their time.

The costs of control can become more complex when the connections among issues cross agency boundaries. To continue with the example, suppose that while the housing administrators are acting, school administrators are faced with declining enrollments and are deciding whether to close specific schools. A school that has been closed might provide a housing site. New housing, however, might create greater demand for existing schools. What one agency does clearly has consequences for the other. Yet the two agencies are operating under independent constraints imposed by different political actors—the city council in one case, the school board in the other. Neither agency will be able to do its job as well as it might if it is not given discretion to adjust its behavior to the other's actions.[24]

24. Writing about a housing authority, Martin Meyerson and Edward C. Banfield argue that prior decisions made by other agencies were a critical fact of life: "The opportunity area within which the staff could devise courses of

Connections among issues may pose particularly high costs when there is a lapse in time between the initial imposition of constraint and the other issues on which it has an impact. Constraints are formulated in response to a perceived set of needs, interests, and demands. With the passage of time, or with the impact of the constraint, these may change, but the constraint, once imposed, persists.[25] To return briefly to our hypothetical housing authority, let us suppose that the state government has authorized it to provide a recreation program for teenagers, but has limited participation to those youths who actually live on housing authority property. Let us further suppose that the authority develops a successful program for one of its largest projects, but finds, several months later, that the limits on participation have caused considerable resentment among adolescents living in the neighborhood. The resentment climaxes in fights among rival groups of youths and acts of vandalism to the project. At this point the recreation program has become less of a success and a whole new set of problems for the maintenance staff has been created. Without the ability to change the eligibility requirements for the recreation program, the effectiveness of two areas of housing authority activity will be impaired.

The complexity of modern society makes it virtually impossible to disconnect issues from one another. The only real avenue for solving the problem of interconnectedness is therefore to give bureaucrats greater dis-

---

action was thus circumscribed by decisions which did not arise out of a single clear and consistent intention and which were mostly made by actors who had little or no communication with each other" (*Politics, Planning and the Public Interest* [New York: Free Press, 1955], pp. 269–70).

25. Furthermore, an earlier constraint may limit not only the future behavior of a bureaucrat, but also the future ability of political actors to formulate and impose new constraints in response to new situations (Kaufman, *Red Tape*, p. 27).

cretion, so that they have room in which to maneuver with one another and in response to changing circumstances. Given enough room, however, bureaucrats verge on being under only their own control; and the effort to avoid the costs of control recreates the original problem that control was intended to solve.

Conflicts among Goals

When bureaucrats are faced with a set of issues that embody conflicting goals, a new source of complications for enforcing control may arise.[26] Conflicting goals are likely to be translated into contradictory constraints. Contradictory constraints in turn may be used as an excuse for noncompliance with any given constraint and so bring their own enforcement costs. Herbert Kaufman suggests that "in any large organization, subordinates inevitably receive clashing and contradictory cues and signals from above. . . . Despite efforts to reconcile instructions, many directives come down without regard to those from other sources. When this happens, subordinates may have to decide for themselves what their situations require, picking and choosing among the directives for justification."[27]

Conflicts among the goals of a bureaucracy's control-

26. Edward C. Banfield argues that end structures of public agencies are particularly complex because they are expected to take a wide range of contextual and incidental issues into account. He contrasts them to private organizations, which are generally free to pursue a limited number of primary ends (Banfield, "Notes on Conceptual Scheme," in Meyerson and Banfield, *Politics, Planning and the Public Interest*, p. 321).
27. Kaufman, *Administrative Feedback*, pp. 2–3. "When tasks compete, resources are limited, and the capacity of those in authority to monitor compliance in all aspects of performance is limited, policy implementers have latitude to choose among objectives," Michael Lipsky similarly argues ("Standing the Study of Public Policy Implementation on its Head," in Walter Dean Burnham and Martha Wagner Weinberg, eds., *American Politics and Public Policy* [Cambridge MA: MIT Press, 1978], p. 400).

lers may also create effectiveness problems for the agency. If, rather than ignoring some constraints, bureaucrats choose to try to do contradictory things simultaneously, their effectiveness in doing any of them is likely to be seriously diminished. School administrators, for example, have been told both to maintain racial balance in their classrooms and to provide bilingual education. Since the latter virtually requires a racially imbalanced classroom to allow teaching in Spanish or Chinese, even the most conscientious administrator is likely to stumble in meeting both constraints.

Conflict among policy goals clearly has deleterious effects on the enterprise of control. If goal conflicts are not resolved, the intended effects of control mechanisms are likely to be distorted. Unfortunately, there is no simple formula for resolving conflicts. If there were, the problem would not pervade so many aspects of political life.[28] We may, however, think of three basic strategies for dealing with goal conflict in the context of constraining bureaucratic behavior. These are: to opt for centralized resolution, to partition off sectors and have each decide its own goals, and to leave it to the bureaucrats. Each strategy provides some measure of relief from the problem of goal conflict, but each also takes its toll.

In a centralized strategy, citizens decide upon goals collectively, or through their representatives in legislatures, and then constrain bureaucrats accordingly. This strategy has the appeal of seeming to confront the problem directly, but it in fact begs the question. Goal conflict exists

---

28. As I have noted several times, there are analogies between the problem of democratic control of bureaucracy and the problem of political representation. On the question of goal conflict, Charles E. Gilbert, writing about representation, similarly comments that the concept ignores the problem of aggregating interests (Gilbert, "Operative Doctrines of Representation," *American Political Science Review* 62 [1963]: 616).

because citizens or their representatives cannot agree. Ignoring the conflict may result in an extreme case of either enforcement or effectiveness problems.

Since the control that bureaucrats might have over their own behavior is shifted elsewhere, constraining bureaucrats means redistributing power, and when there is conflict over goals, the stakes are particularly high. The more behavior is constrained, the more power is redistributed, and hence the more people are likely to fight over how bureaucrats should be constrained.[29] One potential result of such fighting is that enforcement of constraint may be nonexistent because of disputes over who gets to control the control mechanism. The experiences of the Ocean Hill–Brownsville community control experiment in New York City, as well as those of numerous community action agencies, are striking examples of how this may happen. The details of these cases vary, but in all of them elected community boards were created as a means of controlling local bureaucracies. These boards were, however, frequently hobbled by warring factions that often seemed more interested in controlling the board than in controlling the bureaucracy.[30] Meanwhile the bureaucracies continued to go about their business, using public power with little guidance from the elected institutions created to control them.

When goal conflict is less intense, it may be moved within the confines of the controlling institutions and power parcelled out to the contending factions. If differ-

---

29. The severity of political conflict increases as the stakes increase, Robert A. Dahl argues (*Democracy in the United States*, 2d ed. [Chicago: Rand McNally, 1972], p. 303).
30. On Ocean Hill–Brownsville, see, for example, Maurice R. Berube and Marilyn Gittell, eds., *Confrontation at Ocean Hill–Brownsville* (New York: Praeger, 1969). On community action agencies, see Moynihan, *Maximum Feasible Misunderstanding*, chap. 7, and James L. Sundquist, *Making Federalism Work* (Washington DC: Brookings Institution, 1969), chap. 2.

ences remain unresolved, however, parcelling out power is an invitation to the contending factions to develop inconsistent and incompatible constraints.[31] This in turn, of course, can create serious costs to effectiveness.[32] Any bureaucrat faced with administering a program passed by Congress but funded through the appropriations process at a fraction of the level necessary to achieve the program's goals can testify to the difficulties this situation can cause. If there is enough parcelling out of power, the centralized strategy is in fact transformed into a sectoral one.

A sectoral strategy for resolving goal conflict accepts the existence of conflict and the difficulty of resolving it. Instead of forcing comprehensive decisions, it opts for dividing society into a series of relatively homogeneous sectors, or interest groups, and allows each to exert moderate constraint over the bureaucrats whose actions most affect the group.[33] In theory such a strategy should allow for effective servicing of group needs, while still allowing

31. "The factors of perennial legislative-executive rivalry, low party cohesion, and limited control by Congress of its own committees permit legislative control of administration to be used as a strategy in the continuous struggle among political, economic, regional and personal interest groups for power and legislative achievement," Joseph P. Harris writes (*Congressional Control of Administration* [Washington DC: Brookings Institution, 1964], p. 7).

32. For example, in a study of urban renewal in Birmingham, England, and Lyon, France, Jerry A. Webman found that high levels of participation in decision making led to less effective plan fulfillment (Webman, *Reviving the Industrial City* [New Brunswick NJ: Rutgers University Press, 1982], chap. 4).

33. "To the extent that hierarchy is weak, conveys no firm consensus, and thus allows discretion in subsystems of interacting strategic centers, then democratic control can be maintained only through influences in the strategic subsystem centers," argues Emmette S. Redford (*Democracy in the Administrative State* [New York: Oxford University Press, 1969], p. 195). In its strongest form this has been called *clientela* by Joseph LaPalombara (*Interest Groups in Italian Politics* [Princeton: Princeton University Press, 1964], chap. 8). He writes: "The *clientela* relationship exists when an interest group, for whatever reasons, succeeds in becoming, in the eyes of a given administrative agency, the natural expression and representative of a given social sector which, in turn, constitutes the natural target or reference point for the activity of the administrative agency" (p. 262).

some latitude for influence by other sectoral interests or by the society as a whole.

In fact, this strategy often fulfills the first expectation but precludes the second. As many have noted, close client relations may lead either to the cooptation of an agency by a client group[34] or to the creation of insulated self-governing systems that allow control only by the groups involved.[35] Thus, even when there is substantial agreement among others over how the agency should be constrained, implementation of an appropriate constraint may be impossible if the sectoral group does not consent.[36] Consequently, a new twist to the enforcement problem arises—namely, intervention by veto groups who block the implementation of constraint. Veterans Administration officials who try to comply with presidential efforts to cut spending are, for example, likely to find their power undermined by the significant control service organizations wield over the agency. A recent agency head was virtually forced out of office by just such circumstances.[37]

34. The phenomenon of cooptation is especially characteristic of regulatory agencies. See Murray Edelman, *The Symbolic Uses of Politics* (Urbana IL: University of Illinois Press, 1964), and Roger C. Noll, *Reforming Regulation* (Washington DC: Brookings Institution, 1971), chap. 3. J. Lieper Freeman describes how bureaucrats and clients come to resemble each other in "The Political Ecology of a Bureau," in Altshuler, ed., *Politics of the Federal Bureaucracy*.

35. This case is perhaps most forcefully made by Theodore Lowi in *The End of Liberalism* (New York: Norton, 1969), especially in chaps. 3 and 4. In his study of the TVA, Philip Selznick found that when an agency worked closely with certain groups, it led to a "freezing of social relations" (Selznick, *TVA and the Grass Roots* [New York: Harper and Row, 1966], p. 112).

36. Dahl and Lindblom explain that "bureaucratic leaders are participants in a bargaining process . . . allies cannot be had for nothing; bureaucratic leaders bargain with suitable rewards: loyalty, information, remission of penalties, projects or a host of other alternatives. As a result, the ties with one group of politicians often become so strong that prescribed superiors in another group are unable to exert effective control" (*Politics, Economics and Welfare*, pp. 342–43).

37. See *National Journal* 14, no. 41 (October 9, 1982): 1715–18.

Furthermore, a sectoral strategy often achieves only limited effectiveness. A sectorally controlled agency may be very effective from the perspective of the sector involved but not at all effective in the view of others who may be affected by agency actions. This problem is particularly serious in the case of regulatory agencies, organizations that have often been accused of serving the interests of the regulated more than those of the consumers,[38] but it is not confined to them. Just as a societal strategy works best when conflicts can be resolved, a sectoral strategy has low costs only when sectors can be partitioned. Otherwise, goal conflict continues, but is perforce resolved in favor of the chosen sector.

A final strategy, that of letting bureaucrats themselves reconcile conflicting goals, is also premised on the difficulty of resolving conflict, but here the solution is not to parcel off bureaucracies but to let the bureaucrats deal with the conflicts as they see fit.[39] In this way the problems latent in the other two strategies are presumably avoided because the bureaucrats are free to formulate coherent and consistent policies. Furthermore, proponents assert that this strategy has the advantage of facilitating important policies, such as the construction of new public housing, that otherwise might be unpopular.[40] The major

38. This accusation is summarized in Kaufman, *Red Tape*, pp. 16–18.
39. As Redford writes, "by establishment of machinery with looser direction, we can have activity for continuous adjustment and choice among interests" (*Democracy in the Administrative State*, p. 195). Arthur Maass also argues that one of the primary reasons for granting administrators discretion is so that they may reconcile interests (Maass, *Muddy Waters* [Cambridge MA: Harvard University Press, 1951], pp. 3–4).
40. Discussing public housing in Chicago, Meyerson and Banfield argue that "it was just as well for the cause of public housing, perhaps, that the politicians did not put the issue before the public in a clearcut way. If they had succeeded in making public opinion consistent, it would have been by splitting into two camps that sizeable sector of it which wanted ends which were empir-

problem created by this strategy is that it involves moving decisions from the political to the bureaucratic arena.[41] This may come perilously close to precisely the situation that the process of constraining bureaucrats was intended to avoid.

There is no single best strategy for coping with goal conflict, just as there is no single answer to the question of how bureaucracies should be democratically controlled. The answer to each question is contingent on one's idea of democracy. The three strategies for dealing with goal conflict—centralized, sectoral, and bureaucratic—are closely related to the various assumptions about citizen ability discussed in chapter 2. As a result, each is linked to a region of our map and closely associated with certain forms of control. Resolution of goal conflict through a centralized strategy lies in the region of high constraint, resolution through a sectoral strategy in the region of moderate constraint, and resolution through a bureaucratic strategy in the region of weak constraint.

In choosing among ways to control bureaucrats, citizens and elected officials must take into account the difficulties of exercising control. Control cannot be achieved without cost. In the effort to restrict the discretion of bureaucrats, citizens and their representatives may pay a price in the

---

ically irreconcilable. And if such a split had occurred, opinion might have crystallized against slum clearance, not for it. It was because many passive supporters of public housing did not realize its implications for their other ends that any compromise at all was possible" (*Politics, Planning and the Public Interest*, p. 255).

41. As Dahl and Lindblom argue, "if political leadership is not agreed, then to shift a decision on major policy to the bureaucracies is typically only to shift the locus of bargaining. If this is not the case, it can only mean that bureaucracies either are not controlled by political leaders or are somehow insulated from all but one segment of them" (*Politics, Economics and Welfare*, p. 350).

effectiveness of the agency involved, in the expenditure of their own time and energy, and in their future ability to exercise control. This price varies, depending on the mechanism of control that is used, the extent that the control reverberates to other issues, and the goal conflict surrounding control. The cost to bureaucratic effectiveness derives largely from an imbalance between the abilities of bureaucrats and those of their controllers. As we shall see in chapter 5, the extent of that imbalance varies across policy areas. Enforcement costs derive from the fact that bureaucrats do not always willingly follow their controllers. To better understand that unwillingness, we must turn to the bureaucrats themselves and to how they look at the issue of controlling bureaucracies.

4

WHO, ME?—THE BUREAUCRATS LOOK AT THE ISSUE OF DEMOCRATIC CONTROL

Bureaucratic decision making creates a challenge for democratic political institutions because the world of democracy and the world of bureaucracy clash in a critical way. Democracy is premised on self-governance, whereas bureaucracies are populated by appointed officials whose power derives from their expertise and institutional position, not from the mandate of the electorate. Until now my vantage point has been that of the world of democracy. I have examined the democratic norms implicit in various control strategies, and I have explored the costs to the would-be controller of exerting various forms of control. As long as the issue of democratic control of bureaucracy is viewed solely through the eyes of the controller, however, our understanding will be incomplete. It will ignore insights derived from the other world involved in the clash: the world of bureaucracy.

In the next three chapters I shift my vantage point from the world of democracy to the world of bureaucracy. These three chapters introduce two major complications to the map I have developed of strategies for democratic control. The first complication consists of the addition of

another perspective to that of the would-be controller—
the perspective of the bureaucrat. The second complication consists of introducing the consequences of differences among policy areas. By adding these two complications I add two more layers of complexity to the
question of choice among control mechanisms. I argue
that the would-be controller should consider both the attitudes of the bureaucrats and the nature of the policy
area in choosing a control strategy. But while complicat-
ing the would-be controller's choice, an understanding of
bureaucratic attitudes and policy area variations also suggests avenues for designing strategies of democratic control more effectively.

In this chapter I begin my examination of bureaucratic
attitudes by discussing how bureaucrats justify their resistance to external control. In chapter 5 I step back from
the bureaucrats themselves and discuss the ways in which
the world they work in varies by policy area; I also discuss
how these variations affect the would-be controller's
choice of control strategy. In chapter 6 I return to the
bureaucrats to examine how variations in the world of
work create variations in bureaucratic perceptions of the
world of democratic politics, and thus create opportunities for bureaucrats to accept some forms of control.

All strategies for controlling bureaucracies are dependent to some extent on the acquiescence of the bureaucrats involved.[1] Opposition will at best force the would-
be controller to expend extra resources on the control

1. Herbert Kaufman, focusing primarily on internal control issues, argues
that "subordinates may know precisely what is expected of them, be perfectly
capable of doing it, and still not do it. What they are asked to do may offend
their personal principles or their interpretation of professional ethics or their
extraorganizational loyalties and commitments or their self interest. . . . When
orders from above conflict sharply with their values, they quietly construe the
orders in a way that makes them tolerable" (Kaufman, *Administrative Feedback*
[Washington DC: Brookings Institution, 1973], pp. 3–4).

effort, at worst lead to the failure of the control effort to constrain bureaucratic behavior. Scholars of bureaucracy have long noted that far from welcoming external intervention, bureaucrats typically resist it.[2] These scholars have generally explained the displeasure bureaucrats express at intrusions into their domain by relying on explanations rooted in the ways institutional structures provide incentives for self-serving behavior. Bureaucrats resist control because they enjoy autonomy, because their lives are easier if they are their own masters, because they feel that they know best.[3]

There is little reason to dispute this portrait of the self-serving bureaucrat. Surely this kind of motivation lies behind bureaucratic resistance to control. But a picture that looks exclusively at bureaucracies per se is incomplete. Bureaucrats are both workers in a bureaucratically structured organization and citizens of a democracy. Thus they are subjected not only to the incentives of the agency but also to the norms of the democracy.[4] A complete under-

2. James D. Thompson, for example, argues that organizations seek to buffer themselves against the outside world (Thompson, *Organizations in Action* [New York: McGraw-Hill, 1967], p. 20). Anthony Downs notes the strong bureaucratic preference for stasis, particularly in the face of external efforts to alter the status quo: "Bureaus have a powerful tendency to continue doing today whatever they did yesterday," he writes (Downs, *Inside Bureaucracy* [Boston: Little, Brown 1967], p. 195). And Robert K. Merton argues that "bureaucratic officials . . . resist change in established routines; at least those changes which are felt to be imposed by others" (Merton, *Social Theory and Social Structure* [Glencoe IL: Free Press, 1957], p. 201).

3. Merton writes of a bureaucratic "pride of craft" that leads bureaucrats to resist change (*Social Theory and Social Structure*, p. 201). Hugh Heclo emphasizes a disposition to reduce "the agonies of change." (Heclo, *A Government of Strangers* [Washington DC: Brookings Institution, 1977], p. 143). Downs suggests that bureaucratic inertia stems from the fact "that established processes represent an enormous previous investment in time, effort and money" (*Inside Bureaucracy*, p. 195).

4. Others have noted the importance of democratic beliefs. Robert A. Dahl, for example, argues that "the extent to which structural changes can achieve their ostensible purposes is severely limited by the civic orientations of citizens and leaders" (Dahl, *Dilemmas of Pluralist Democracy* [New Haven: Yale University Press, 1982], p. 133). "In short, the outlook for democracy depends on the

standing of bureaucratic attitudes toward the issue of
democratic control therefore requires both looking in-
ward at the agency and outward to society.

My goal in this chapter is to explain how bureaucrats
reconcile the conflict between their two roles.[5] I begin by
demonstrating that the bureaucrats I spoke with do not
reject traditional conceptions of democracy, although
they seek isolation from the political process. I then proceed to examine how bureaucrats are able to hold such
seemingly contradictory beliefs.[6] I am not trying to assess
the validity of the positions bureaucrats take. Rather, I
am trying to understand in detail what their perspectives
are. If these perspectives were as varied as the individuals
involved, they might be of interest, but would be of little
use. This is not the case. There are patterns to bureaucratic beliefs, patterns that are attributable to the daily
experiences of bureaucrats on the job.[7] An understand-

---

commitment of bureaucrats and politicians to democratic principles," Joel D.
Aberbach, Robert D. Putnam, and Bert A. Rockman contend (*Bureaucrats and
Politicians in Western Democracies* [Cambridge MA: Harvard University Press,
1981], pp. 170–71). Robert Jervis more generally argues for the importance of
bureaucratic perceptions as a determinant of bureaucratic behavior (Jervis,
Perception and Misperception in International Politics [Princeton: Princeton University Press, 1976]).

5. For a general discussion of the issue of how belief systems arise to resolve
role conflicts and then have an impact on how those conflicts continue to be
resolved, see Peter L. Berger and Thomas Luckmann, *The Social Construction of
Reality* (Garden City NY: Doubleday, Anchor Books, 1967).

6. Robert D. Putnam's findings on the normative beliefs of members of
Parliament in Great Britain and Italy support the expectation that there should
be a relationship between attitudes about democracy and attitudes about control. He found that "the relationship between models of democracy and attitudes toward popular participation . . . shows a neat and unbroken progression
as one moves along the continuum from authoritarian democrats to polyarchal
and liberal democrats to classical democrats. Respondents at each step along
this continuum advocate a higher and higher level of involvement and influence for members of the mass public" (Putnam, *The Beliefs of Politicians* [New
Haven: Yale University Press, 1973], p. 203).

7. Michael Lipsky makes a forceful argument in *Street-Level Bureaucracy*
(New York: Russell Sage Foundation, 1980) for the importance of daily work
routines in shaping bureaucratic practice and belief.

ing of these patterns in the way bureaucrats think about the issue of democratic control will reveal both paths toward improving the prospects for such control and pitfalls that might otherwise go unnoticed.

In order to look at the issue of democratic control through the eyes of the bureaucrat, I conducted a study of the attitudes of local bureaucrats. The subjects of my study were thirty-nine administrators who worked for the housing authority, fire department, or board of education in a moderate-sized northeastern city. In 1980 the city had a population of approximately 125,000, about one-third of whom were black and under 10 percent Hispanic; the median family income was about $15,000 a year. Almost 20 percent of the families had incomes below the poverty level.[8] The city is governed by an elected mayor and by a city council selected in a partisan election on a district basis. During the interview period the majority of the council and the mayor were Democrats; a Republican subsequently assumed the mayoralty. Each of the agencies studied has a board appointed by the mayor that oversees agency affairs. Board members serve for fixed, staggered terms. The education and fire departments receive virtually all of their funds from the city budget, and the housing authority is funded largely from federal and, to a lesser extent, state funds.

I talked to all major central office decision makers, as well as to randomly selected chief field administrators (principals in education, deputy chiefs in fire, project directors in housing).[9] In education and housing the chief

8. United States Department of Commerce, Bureau of the Census, *1980 Census of Population: Social and Economic Characteristics* (Washington DC: Government Printing Office), vol. 8.

9. In education I spoke with the superintendent, the assistant superintendents, the directors (of personnel, elementary schools, middle schools, secondary and continuing education, adult education, pupil services, special projects)

administrator is hired by the board and can be dismissed only for cause during the course of the contract. The other respondents are career officials. All of the people I spoke with have considerable responsibility and authority. Most of the central office officials have administrative or technical staff working for them, and the field administrators have primary responsibility for delivering the agency's services. These are the people who design their agency's programs and oversee their implementation, who develop the agency's budget and negotiate with other government officials to obtain the necessary funds, who diagnose and solve problems in the agency as they arise. In other words, these are all people who make policy.

I chose to study local bureaucrats because in many ways they are the frontline troops in the battle for democratic control. The services they deliver may not be the most globally important, but they have an immediacy to people's daily lives that often leads citizens to care passionately about what an agency does, and to feel close enough to the agency to make their concerns known.[10] During the period in which I conducted my interviews, each of these agencies was caught in a web of pressures from the mayor, council, community groups, client groups, and individual citizens over such issues as budget cuts, contracts for agency personnel, the adequacy of services in various neighborhoods, specific personnel decisions, school closings, class size, discipline, eviction procedures, lease pro-

---

and several principals. In the fire department I spoke with the chief, the assistant chiefs, the deputy chiefs, the fire marshal, the deputy marshal, and the supervisors (of motor apparatus and building facilities). In housing I spoke with the executive director, the assistant directors, the directors (of maintenance, police, and projects for the elderly), the controller, and the managers of several specific programs (housing development, section 8, tenant management).

10. See Douglas Yates, *The Ungovernable City* (Cambridge MA: MIT Press, 1977), for an elaboration of this argument.

visions, and the quality of arson investigations. These pressures were amply reported in the local newspapers and reflected in the comments of the people I spoke with. Interviewing thirty-nine people is clearly an exercise in hypothesis generation, not hypothesis testing. I selected respondents with an eye to obtaining a range of attitudes, not to creating a sample that could confidently be generalized to a larger universe. I chose the specific agencies I did because I thought they would provide variation on some of the dimensions I expected to be important in determining attitudes and in conditioning responses to control efforts by various political actors. The people I spoke with differed considerably in terms of such things as education, professionalization, the technical complexity of their jobs, and community support for the work of their agency.[11]

Several factors suggest, however, that the patterns of belief I uncovered were not atypical. Despite the fact that my respondents varied in age, education, and background both within and across agencies, the similarity of their beliefs on many issues is striking. Furthermore, my interviews were conducted during a time of political transition in the city involved. As a result, in spite of their working in the same city, the political connections and loyalties of these bureaucrats were far from homogeneous. They were a mixed group whom it would be hard to call typical of the bureaucrats in a certain kind of city. Some had risen through the ranks; others had come into the agency laterally. Some had ties to an old-style ethnic political organization, some to newer "reform" leaders, and others virtually no local political ties at all.

The interviews themselves consisted of a series of

---

11. A full discussion of the nature of variation among these agencies and the consequences of it is the focus of chapter 6.

open-ended questions[12] about the individual's background, attitudes toward his or her job, the nature of his
or her work, patterns of influence over agency affairs,
attitudes about the proper role of various political actors
in local decision making, attitudes about the general
problem of democratic control of bureaucracy, and about
the individual's conception of democracy.[13] The interviews ranged in length from an hour to two and a half
hours. Everyone contacted granted me an interview.

Overall, these interviews paint a challenging picture
for those concerned with democratic control of bureaucracy. The bureaucrats not only describe themselves as
being relatively free from such control, they also do not
perceive much of a need for it. In their world the role of
bureaucrats as political actors pales in comparison with
the role of bureaucrats as people on the job. They see the
strictures of democracy as being applicable to others, but
not to themselves. They do, however, believe in those
strictures; they espouse fairly classic democratic norms.
But the bureaucrats manage to construct a view of their
own situation such that, even when democratic norms
seem applicable, they do not prescribe significant constraints on bureaucratic behavior.

AUTONOMOUS BUREAUCRATS, DEMOCRATIC CITIZENS

The bureaucrats I spoke with consider themselves to have
significant latitude of action, and they like it that way. The

12. For a discussion of the use of open-ended interviews for this kind of
research, see Joel D. Aberbach, James D. Chesney, and Bert A. Rockman, "Ex-
ploring Elite Political Attitudes: Some Methodological Lessons," *Political Meth-
odology* 2 (1975): 1–28.
13. A copy of the interview schedule appears as Appendix I. All but three
of the interviews were tape recorded. All were then coded from transcripts
either of the tapes or of notes taken during and immediately after the interviews. Coding was checked by a second person, who read a random sample of
the transcripts with no appreciably different result.

weight of external control that they feel either through orders or, more subtly, through influence is slight. Thirty of the thirty-nine report that they "feel pretty much free to do what they want to do on the job."[14] A school administrator explained, "I personally feel that I do have a great deal of freedom on the job in terms of making decisions about children, in terms of running the operation here." And from a housing administrator I heard, "I have the ability and the authority to operate the department as I see fit, as long as it conforms to the general goals and objectives of the authority itself." When asked who else had influence over department policy, only seven of the administrators said the mayor; fewer still said clients, the public, or other politicians.

These perceptions of freedom do not mean that the bureaucrats are totally unconstrained by outside forces. Consciously or not, the bureaucrats surely realize that there are certain types of behavior that would invite mayoral, council, or citizen response. Yet on a day-to-day basis these bureaucrats are clearly acting within the weak constraints such limits create.

Whether the resulting discretion is seen as excessive depends on one's view of democracy (as discussed in chapter 2) and on the desires of the other political actors involved. If this form of weak constraint were all that the mayor, the council, or the citizens ever wanted to impose, the bureaucrats would be under firm democratic control. On the other hand, if these actors sought to tighten or change the constraint, the issue would become whether the bureaucrats would accept this. To use Chester Barnard's famous phrase, the question is whether the bureaucrats are working within the citizenry's "zone of indifference" or whether the citizens are operating within

14. All the data reported in this chapter are for the sample as a whole. Policy area effects will be discussed in the next chapter. Some quotations have been slightly changed to disguise the identity of the respondent or the city.

that of the bureaucrats.[15] The answer to that question is suggested by the bureaucrats' description of how they think influence ought to be distributed.

Most of the bureaucrats I spoke with prefer outside actors to have very little power. When asked, "Who do you think has a right to a say about what goes on in your department?" the most commonly cited outside groups were those affected by decisions (clients, parents, tenants); but even such groups were mentioned by less than a third of the respondents. The community was included by ten, the board by six, and the mayor by only five. These figures probably indicate even greater unwillingness to allow outside influence than they at first suggest, since during the course of most of the interviews it became clear that the bureaucrats interpreted "say" very loosely as "complain" or "make their ideas known," and not necessarily as "constrain agency activities."

Each of the bureaucrats was also asked to describe the kind of role he or she thought the board, the mayor, and the public should play in the operation of the department. For the board, the bureaucrats sought the reverse of what is formally prescribed. Twenty-eight of the thirty-nine thought the board should merely react to agency proposals. A fire administrator told me his ideal role for the board would be one of "helping the chief efficiently run the department," and a housing administrator said of the board, "They can help in getting funds. They can be supportive when the problems come in." A school administrator was more expansive in describing his preferred role for the board: "I'd prefer to see the board show its confidence in the superintendent and his advisory staff, or in his total staff, and be inclined to take action on pro-

15. Chester I. Barnard, *The Functions of the Executive* (Cambridge MA: Harvard University Press, 1938), chap. 12.

posals that have been professionally developed, [that have had] professional imprimatur, if you will, put on them and then [been] brought to the board for their consideration, review and attention." For the overwhelming majority of the administrators, the ideal is a board that basically serves the department, not the reverse.

Mayoral influence is even less welcome. Only five of those interviewed advocated active mayoral involvement in departmental affairs. The rest were fairly evenly split between those wanting the mayor merely to cooperate (seventeen) and those wanting no mayoral involvement at all (sixteen).[16] The former view was typified by a housing administrator who said he thought the mayor and council members "should play a supportive role" and by the school administrator who told me, "I think there should be a cooperative kind of relationship so that we can understand what their problems are, carry out our responsibilities and also listen to what they feel is necessary." The latter, more closed view is reflected in the comments of an educator who said, "My feeling is that there shouldn't be any political influence on the schools," and of a housing administrator who told me, "Practically, I would say that it's easier to do a good job if the local political control is not there."

There was only slightly greater support for a role for the community, with about a third of the administrators reporting that some input short of decision making was appropriate. An educator described his preferred role for the public this way: "I think there should be input, appropriate input. Not necessarily on decision-making levels, but certainly on the collection of information and opinion." A fire administrator talked of a similarly limited

16. Figures do not always total thirty-nine because some respondents did not answer all questions.

role for the public: "Oh, the public. Well, you certainly don't deny them having their input into it. . . . We would certainly honor any request that any citizen has. We would listen to them, try to answer their question." Two-thirds of the administrators advocated still more limited roles for the public—that is, either "being supportive" or no role at all. A housing administrator explained the former position: "Well, I think the general public has a dual role, that of being supportive of public housing . . . and also the role of informing one another of what public housing is and the fact that it is a type of housing that cannot be excluded from certain neighborhoods." A fire administrator typifies those who advocated no role for the public at all. He told me, "You just can't take people off the street and say 'Okay, we're going to give you a hand in running the department.'" Thus, whether the subject is the mayor, the board, the city council, or the public, these interviews strongly portray a group of bureaucrats who see power over agency affairs confined within the agency, and who believe that this is the way it should be, a happy situation for a bureaucrat, perhaps, but not for those concerned with democratic decision making.

A very different picture emerges, however, when the topic shifts from a discussion of an individual agency to beliefs about democracy. In spite of their distaste for outside intervention, these bureaucrats do not reject traditional conceptions of democracy. When I asked them about what they see as the essentials of a democracy, they raised the classic themes of self-governance and freedom. A fire administrator put it simply: "Government by the people, for the people. That's what it means." The sentiment was echoed by a school administrator. "You tell the politicians what to do. You elect your own officials. You vote them out when you want to vote them out." A colleague took this idea even further. "The Declaration of

Independence. It's an organization that provides government in which the consent of the governed plays a very, very strong role. And that's in all areas, not only in taxation or legislation."

Others stressed liberty. A housing administrator said of democracy, "I think I go along with the Constitution on that. The right to the pursuit of happiness, free speech, those kinds of things." A school administrator held democracy to mean that "I'm free to worship where I wish and free to vote as I wish." Often the themes were joined, as they were by a housing administrator. "I suppose equal protection. That a person be accorded the same rights or privileges no matter who he is, how much money he has, or doesn't have, where he lives. A democracy really has to protect the rights of the few while doing what the majority feels right."

These are hardly the words of people who question traditional democratic teachings. Only nine of the bureaucrats I spoke with raised the idea that a democracy required a government with a role independent of its citizens, and in every case this was qualified by the statement that government should be responsive. Furthermore, when asked, "Are there ways that this city or country could or should be more democratic than it is today?" only one person suggested that less popular participation would be desirable. In fact, the most common reform suggested (by eight people) was that popular participation be increased. Typical of such suggestions was that from a school administrator who told me, "You have to listen more. More input from the people." Others suggested electoral reform, greater socioeconomic equality, reducing corruption, and reducing corporate power.[17]

17. Similar patterns of belief have been found by other researchers. Joel Aberbach and Bert Rockman found that a majority of American federal executives were sympathetic to increasing the role of citizen activities, although

Support for the basic tenets of democracy does not, however, necessarily produce an appreciation of how those tenets are translated into the actual workings of government. In fact, the bureaucrats I spoke with seemed almost blissfully unaware that their desire for autonomy might conflict with democratic values. Fairly late in the interviews I asked, "Some people talk about public agencies being undemocratic. Do you think that this is a problem?" The response was strongly, "No." Fewer than a third said they thought such a problem existed. Since further conversation revealed that many of these were not talking about control at all, this probably overstates the number who saw the contradiction between democracy and bureaucratic decision making. A school administrator, for example, said that he thought there was a problem with public agencies being undemocratic, and explained, "That means you're not sensitive to people's needs." His proposed solution to the problem was simple: "Someone calls and you answer the telephone. You talk to them." Similarly, a housing administrator proposed "proper communication, notification, considering your fellow man" as ways to make public agencies more democratic. And a fire administrator, who thought his agency was in fact very democratic, offered this example: "We're very democratic around here. We try very hard to be part of the public. We, I think, sometimes even bend over backwards. For example, the guys take up donations to help fire victims." Answering phone calls and helping fire

---

few of them had no reservations about the proposition ("Administrators' Beliefs About the Role of the Public: The Case of American Federal Executives," *Western Political Quarterly* 31 [December 1978]: 510). Aberbach, Putnam, and Rockman report on the beliefs about the role of the public held by European bureaucrats. They found that 44 percent of them were either rather or very favorable to increasing popular control or citizen participation and that only 16 percent of them thought that the role of the public should be confined to voting or less (*Bureaucrats and Politicians*, pp. 182–83).

victims may be desirable, but the fact that these were the primary examples of the democratic nature of public agencies these bureaucrats could offer testifies to the weakness of their conception of the ways democracy interacts with their work.

Approaching the question of democratic control from a different direction, I asked the bureaucrats whether they felt public agencies were too responsive to outside pressures and groups. The answers give further evidence that on an intellectual level the bureaucrats do not see the need for greater democratic control. Almost half of the administrators felt that excessive responsiveness was not a problem, but only because agencies could hold their own against outside pressures. As a fire administrator flatly said, "We don't get pushed around." A housing administrator was gentler, but made a similar point: "Responding, but not necessarily giving in, is what I see going on here, and I think that's healthy." Only two bureaucrats said they felt public agencies were not responsive enough. One-third replied that public agencies were already too responsive. A fire administrator stated simply, "I think that is a problem. I think they've gone a little too far and too fast, which is not good." A school administrator answered much more personally: "There's no question in my mind we react too much to community pressures. And I think that many decisions that we make are made almost on the spur of the moment in terms of whatever the pressure from the community is." Another school administrator made a similar point: "We have some principals who are so concerned about being open and responsive to everybody that they are really nothing to anybody. They're bounced from pillar to post. They are appeasing this group and that group and the other group. There's no common denominator. There's no pattern. There's no strand, no cohesiveness about any of their actions."

Still a third tack was to raise the specific problem of red tape, a most galling issue to the public, and one that in its saliency and simplicity might be expected to be particularly evocative of responses compatible with democratic concerns. The bureaucrats were not too sympathetic. Only ten said without major qualification that red tape was a problem; four allowed that it might be a problem elsewhere, but not in their own agency; eight said it was not a problem at all; and twelve argued that the rules embodied in red tape were necessary. Characteristic of this last perspective was the housing administrator who explained, "Most of the forms we have to fill out and the procedures we have to go through I think are pretty necessary . . . to ensure that the housing authority runs properly, to ensure that all people are treated fairly, and for our own records, for our own knowledge of what is happening." A fire administrator made a similar argument about red tape: "There are certain ground rules that everyone has to follow . . . sometimes it's important." Thus, regardless of whether the issue of democratic control was raised directly or negatively (and in a weak form—i.e., responsiveness—at that) or by a specific problem, the response of these bureaucrats, who otherwise subscribed to democratic beliefs, seemed to be, "Who, me?"

How can bureaucrats accept democratic principles yet reject their implications? Why is it that bureaucrats do not seem to see a conflict between their normative beliefs and the way they seek to live their daily lives? The answer lies not in a problem with the beliefs, but in the other half of the question, in the daily lives of the bureaucrats. Bureaucrats are not only appointed government officials; they are also people at work. Bureaucratic perspectives on democratic control seem to be affected much more by the ongoing realities of the job than by abstract beliefs.

Such beliefs may be of central importance to the would-be controller's choice of a control strategy, but they are largely irrelevant to the bureaucrat's response.

The conditions bureaucrats work in and their perceptions of those conditions do two things. First, they tend not to raise democratic norms, and thus fail to provide an environment in which these norms can guide behavior. Second, they redefine the first two components of the concept "democratic control of bureaucracy"—that is, democracy and control—in ways that create variances for the specific situation of the individual bureaucrat. These variances then enable bureaucrats to make their opposition to control consistent with democratic beliefs.

THE INSULATED BUREAUCRAT

Bureaucrats are public officials, but they are public officials who do not go through the socializing ritual of the electoral process. They have neither to proclaim American democratic verities in order to keep their jobs nor go through an overtly political process to obtain the jobs in the first place. Thus it should not be surprising if bureaucrats rarely think of themselves as political actors subject to democratic strictures. In fact, the bureaucrats I talked with rarely spoke of themselves as engaged in the political process and almost uniformly failed to connect their work with the operation of a democracy.

"Tell me a little bit about how you see your job," I asked my respondents. Their answers were predictably varied, but two-thirds described themselves in terms that added up to their being administrators. Some listed their specific responsibilities, such as budget preparation, personnel management, maintaining records. Others gave a more general response, like the school administrator who said,

"I have major responsibility for the administration and
supervision of a portion of the schools in this city. . . . I
think one of the main roles I'm involved in is to ensure
that the schools function in an orderly, meaningful educational manner." Two emphasized that they provided a
substantive service, including a school administrator who
replied, "I see my job as more or less giving someone an
opportunity to do or to be what they want to do." A fire
administrator typified a final group of eleven by giving
an affective description: "Well, I enjoy it. I find it exciting
and challenging."

What is most interesting about these responses is that
no one described him or herself as a public official.[18] Only
eleven of the bureaucrats even mentioned the public
when they described their jobs, and only two said anything suggesting that policy was a part of what they did.
In fact, during the course of the interview, three-quarters
of the bureaucrats at some point asserted that they did
not make policy, that policy was made elsewhere. Overall,
then, these bureaucrats do not give the impression of a
group aware of their position in a democratic political
process. In the words of one of my respondents: "I keep
away from politics. Politics are not my cup of tea."

As they see it, the world of bureaucrats is filled with
administrative matters, technical services, substantive
programs and job satisfactions or dissatisfactions—not
with political issues or the search to implement democratic norms. Robert Putnam discusses a related phenomenon in his work on the attitudes of European civil servants. He argues that civil servants "use technical or

18. Robert A. Dahl and Charles E. Lindblom argue that "faulty identification" puts limits on the external control of bureaucracy. The identifications they
discuss are as a professional and as a member of an organization (Dahl and
Lindblom, *Politics, Economics and Welfare* [Chicago: University of Chicago Press,
1976], p. 260).

administrative or financial criteria for defending their preferred policies and for criticizing alternatives. . . . Politicians live in a world of political pressures to be reconciled, while civil servants live in a world of practical problems to be solved."[19]

A self-image of technician or administrator can, of course, be useful for preserving one's autonomy vis-à-vis political leaders. If what one does is not political, then politicians have no business intervening.[20] The obvious expedience of this posture for bureaucrats invites scrutiny and, perhaps, disbelief. But I do not think that this apolitical persona is contrived, a ruse elaborately designed to protect bureaucratic turf. My respondents initially had no idea I was interested in the problem of democratic control. I approached them saying I was doing a study about bureaucratic life and I wanted to interview them about their jobs, phrases purposely meant to be vague. The question asking them to describe their job was one of the first asked, long before any mention was made of mayors, citizens, or democracy. Thus, even if the myth of the apolitical bureaucrat had begun as a ruse, it was one that had become so incorporated into the thought processes of virtually everyone I spoke with that it was expressed in response to the most innocent question. Whether born as a widespread dissimulation or, as I be-

19. Robert D. Putnam, "Bureaucrats and Politicians: Contending Elites in the Policy Process," in *Perspectives on Public Policy Making*, ed. William B. Gwyn and George C. Edwards III, Tulane Studies in Political Science, vol. 15 (New Orleans: Tulane University Press, 1975), pp. 191, 202. Aberbach, Putnam, and Rockman advance a similar argument (*Bureaucrats and Politicians*, chap. 5).

20. Ezra N. Suleiman discusses this in relation to the highest level French administrators. He argues that "the belief that the politician ought not to enter into the details of the work of the Directors reflects a significant self-definition of the civil servant's role: a technician with a monopoly over a domain. A politician either does not infringe upon this monopoly because of his other, more enduring interests, or he cannot because of lack of competence" (Suleiman, *Politics, Power and Bureaucracy in France* [Princeton: Princeton University Press, 1974], p. 231).

lieve more likely, in response to the normal pressures and environment of bureaucratic life, the myth has become genuine belief.

A glimpse at the daily life of these administrators reveals why they think of themselves in this way; there is little to remind them that they are, in fact, public actors. They rarely communicate with political leaders, and neither do they have much direct contact with them. These bureaucrats thus do not have a substantial opportunity to connect their work with broad questions of politics, much less with democracy.[21] I asked a series of questions about the individual's patterns of communication and interaction, and the answers consistently pointed to insularity within each agency. When asked to whom they talked about their work, the most common response (by twenty-six of the bureaucrats) was other people in the agency. The next most common answer was a relative or friend (given by sixteen of the thirty-nine). In contrast, only two of the bureaucrats mentioned the board; three either the mayor, someone from his office, or a member of the city council; two the community; and three clients. Similarly, when asked whose advice they sought, the answer was rarely elected officials. Rather, it was most commonly others in the agency (by twenty-one) and sometimes fellow professionals (by eight). Only two included the board in their list of those they asked for advice, two included clients, and no one mentioned the mayor or any other political figure. In neither of these questions were the bu-

---

21. Aberbach, Putnam, and Rockman discuss the relationship between bureaucratic contacts and political attitudes from the other direction, that of the bureaucrat whose attitudes are unusually close to those of politicians. They found that support for pluralism and for populism is unusually high among those closest to the center of power: "It is as if contacts upward and outward from the bureaucracy remove them from a climate that is less hospitable to democratic ideals and expose them to an atmosphere more like that ordinarily breathed by politicians" (*Bureaucrats and Politicians*, pp. 203–4).

reaucrats forced to make a single choice; they were allowed as many responses as they wanted. Thus the low numbers for contact outside the agency do not reflect those for whom this is the primary source of interaction, but those for whom there is any such reported interaction at all.

The pattern is reinforced from outside as well. I asked the bureaucrats, "Who asks you for advice?" and the answers were virtually the same. Overwhelmingly, the people who ask bureaucrats for advice are other bureaucrats in the same agency. Only one reported that board members asked him for advice; two said the mayor or a member of the city council did; two said citizens. Perhaps not surprisingly, those mentioning a board member, the mayor, or some other public official were almost exclusively agency heads. This is probably the result of a combination of administrative courtesy and good sense that dictates to outsiders that the agency chief not be bypassed. An unfortunate side effect, however, is that a context for allowing administrators in general to feel that they are part of the political system is forfeited because of the inability or unwillingness of political representatives to penetrate the bureaucratic world.

Bureaucratic isolation is also revealed in the bureaucrats' reports of the frequency of their contact with board members, the mayor's office, and members of the city council. Almost half reported that they seldom had contact with the board. Those who did have contact described it as being dominated by requests for specific information and not by discussions of programs or policies. Only three said they ever discussed policy questions with members of the board. In order to explain the paucity of their interactions with the outside, administrators of both the housing authority and the fire department stressed that lines of authority ran through the head of the agency.

But none of the three who reported having policy discussions with board members was an agency head.

Lines of communication with the elected officials of the city are also weak. Six of the bureaucrats reported fairly frequent contact with the mayor's office, but this was virtually always about complaints the mayor had received or about requests for information. A school administrator described his contact with the mayor's office as being "just problems," and a housing administrator told me that her only contact came from the fact that "They write the director all these incredible memos about complaints, and I usually get to answer them." Only six of the administrators reported ever having contact with the mayor about programs or policies.

About half of the bureaucrats reported some interaction with members of the city council, but again the interaction was overwhelmingly about constituent complaints and problems. A housing administrator described his contact with the council as "periodic. And it's mostly when there's trouble." A fire administrator also reported periodic contact: "Some councilmen, because they represent their constituents . . . will say 'Take a look at the building for me. There are some people in my district who are interested in it. If you do, I'll appreciate it.' " A colleague in the fire department reported "no contact, not unless I get calls. At times we have heavy rain storms, or heavy floods, or a condition that a councilman may be trying to correct." Only two of the administrators indicated that they had regular or frequent contact with a member of the council about policy matters. Those lines of communication that do exist primarily concern adjudication or amelioration of specific problems, not policy issues. Such patterns of contact reinforce the bureaucrats' conception of themselves as implementers, not policy makers, since discussions are over narrow details, not broader trends.

THE CONSTRAINED BUREAUCRAT

Daily life on the job may do little to remind bureaucrats that they are public officials who should be democratically controlled, but it also does little to suggest to them that lack of control is a problem. They feel constrained, but not by people outside their agencies.[22] When asked, "Who sets limits on you?" the large majority indicated that limits were derived from within the organization. As a fire administrator told me, "I have the chief to answer to. Anything that comes up as far as a major decision naturally has to be taken to him." A colleague in education described a similar situation: "I do make it a habit of checking with the superintendent, but essentially I can act, and not react." Limits on housing administrators were likewise internal to the agency: "I would say that on any substantive issue there really aren't limits as long as the director knows what I'm doing. Those are more or less the only limits." Only one bureaucrat felt sufficiently unconstrained to say that the primary limits were self-imposed, but only a handful replied that they felt limits from outside the agency—five replied that the board imposed limits and one that the mayor did. Each of the bureaucrats was also asked, "Who do you see yourself as being answerable to?" Only six gave the highly autonomous reply that they felt responsible merely to themselves. Thirty of the thirty-nine reported that they were responsible to

22. See Herbert Kaufman, *Red Tape* (Washington DC: Brookings Institution, 1977) for a description of many of the constraints bureaucrats face.

their superiors in the department. They were allowed to
list as many people as they wanted, but still only four included the mayor, the city council, or any other political
leader, and only thirteen included the board.
If these bureaucrats worked in agencies that approached a classically ordered hierarchical organization
in which all power flowed from the top to the bottom,
these results might not be troubling from a democratic
perspective. The heads of the agencies would be the ones
subject to outside influence, and their subordinates would
feel that influence only as constraint from within the
agency. The control would be substantial enough, moreover, that lower level bureaucrats would exercise little discretion. In fact, however, the agency heads seemed to feel
only slightly more constrained by outside forces than the
other bureaucrats and, while none of the bureaucrats felt
free of constraint, they all reported exercising a fair
amount of discretion. Of the three agencies I studied, the
fire department came closest to the hierarchical model.
Yet the fire chief told me, "I have complete freedom. I
couldn't operate any other way. There is a board of fire
commissioners . . . but they don't make the decisions
about the fire department. They discuss things with me
but they don't make the judgments." The superintendent
of schools reported feeling the influence of the incum-
bent mayor, but saw him as an aberration. Of the previous
administration he reported, "It was such a pleasure to run
the school system. When you don't have interference, it's
beautiful, it's just great." The external constraint felt by
the head of the housing authority came not from citizens
or elected officials, but from other bureaucrats—those in
the federal government.[23]

23. Further doubt is cast on the hypothesis that democratic control flows
through the top of an agency by the fact that none of the six people who reported contact with the mayor's office over policy issues is an agency head.

REDEFINING NORMS

The world in which bureaucrats work may do little to suggest that democratic norms should govern bureaucratic behavior, but bureaucrats are not wholly oblivious to their governmental role. When they do think of it, however, they manage, through a variety of what might be called "sleights of thought," to redefine two key concepts—control and democracy—so that bureaucratic behavior conforms with a newly constituted norm of democratic control of bureaucracy.

Control is dealt with quite simply: it is conceived of in such a manner that its exercise by an outsider does little to constrain what bureaucrats do. One way bureaucrats accomplish this is by accepting the distinction between policy and administration but then defining policy in such a way as to make it an almost empty concept. As noted earlier, the bureaucrats I interviewed overwhelmingly rejected the idea that they made policy. Policy according to them is made elsewhere, usually by the board. If this were true, then democratic control of bureaucracy would be less of a problem. Elected officials or their surrogates on boards and commissions would make policy, and bureaucrats would merely do what flowed from that policy. Unfortunately, as virtually any student of administration knows, it is not so simple to distinguish policy from administration, and neither is it automatic that making "policy" means significantly controlling administrative discretion. This is particularly true when administrators themselves have a large role, as they often do, in determining what falls within the realm of policy, what within that of administration. "Most issues are defined by super-

---

Furthermore, there is no obvious hierarchical logic that would predict who those six are. Overall, the agency heads do not stand out in terms of their patterns of interaction and communication.

intendents as internal, and many boards appear to have difficulty in staking out a legitimate territory," argue Harmon Zeigler and M. Kent Jennings, writing about local educational decision making.[24]

It should come as little surprise to learn that to the bureaucrats I spoke with, policy making is neither a very strenuous activity nor one likely to result in major constraint on administrative behavior. In their eyes, policy making consists of specifying the most general outcomes the agency is to achieve; all the rest is administration. An educational administrator described it nicely in response to a question about the role he saw the board of education playing: "I think that making education policy is their major role. I think the way the system should operate is that they do just that but limit themselves to just that. They make policies and from there on in it becomes administrative." I then asked him for an example of a policy decided by the board. His answer: "Teach kids to read."[25]

A second variation on this theme is that policy making may involve making decisions that impose greater constraint on bureaucratic behavior, but that these are purely reactions to proposals from the administrators themselves. A housing administrator explained: "The board should ratify policies but take no operational role." Another educational administrator was somewhat more expansive. When asked to give an example of policy making

24. Harmon Zeigler and M. Kent Jennings, *Governing American Schools: Political Interaction in Local School Districts* (North Scituate MA: Duxbury Press, 1974), p. 157. See also Frederick M. Wirt and Michael W. Kirst, *Political and Social Foundations of Education* (Berkeley CA: McCutchan, 1975), chap. 5. In *Politics, Planning and the Public Interest* (New York: Free Press, 1955), Martin Meyerson and Edward C. Banfield discuss at some length the ways the Chicago Housing Authority staff influenced policy making by commissioners.

25. Similarly, Zeigler and Jennings argue that superintendents define boards' choices as being either support or firing. Any supervision of the educational program is defined as "being involved in administration" (*Governing American Schools*, p. 190).

by the board, he suggested a situation in which a superintendent met with high school principals and counselors and concluded that the curriculum should be more demanding. The superintendent would then

> propose and recommend to the board that they set a policy that no youngster will graduate from the high school unless he has twenty units instead of sixteen. That's policy. He presents it, they review it, they interrogate him, question him why he wants to do it—back and forth—are there any problems? No? All right, no problems. Then somebody makes a motion "I move we accept this policy and put it in our administrators' manuals." And there's a second, they vote, now it becomes policy.

It may comfort administrators to think that they are not making policy and are therefore immune to the problems of democratic control. But observers who value democratic control will not be appeased. In effect, by granting a board such a limited policy-making role, the administrators are weakening the board's authority, while absolving themselves of charges that they are straying into the political realm, where they agree they do not belong. They thus accept extremely weak externally imposed constraint and reject all other political control as illegitimate.

Administrators have a second way of accepting democratic control by weakening its meaning: they transform control into responsiveness to individuals. The bureaucrats I spoke with had fairly extensive contact with citizens and expressed fairly strong acceptance of the need for it. Over half said that they had either daily or frequent contact with individual citizens or citizen groups, and two-thirds felt that this was an important part of their job. Less than a quarter said that they rarely or never had such contact, and only two suggested that these contacts were a necessary evil. But the nature of the contact was highly particularistic; it did not concern policy issues. Fire ad-

ministrators described telephone calls about air condi-
tioners, bats, fireplaces, sewers, and the fire code. School
administrators talked with parents about specific problems their children were having and with citizens who
lived near schools. Housing administrators fielded tenants' questions about maintenance, evictions, and dam-
ages. By being open to this kind of interaction with citizens and accepting the need for it, administrators are able
to believe they are fulfilling their responsibilities as governmental officials while simultaneously denying external
actors significant control over their behavior.

Equally revealing are the administrators' answers to
questions about why they think contact with citizens and
citizen groups is important. Over and over, the emphasis
was on helping individuals, on being humane. One school
administrator explained, "I think it is very important. If
people take the time to call me or to write to me, they're
in need, they want something, so I feel I should take the
time to answer them." A housing administrator maintained, "I really resent people who put individuals off. I
think that it's important that I develop that kind of rap-
port on an individual basis with people." And from a fire
administrator, "I don't mind it, don't mind it one bit. I
think if they take the time to call up, they feel something
is wrong, and I see nothing wrong with them complaining."

Occasionally someone suggested that such responsiveness was particularly important, since citizens were also
taxpayers, but even these comments reflected a conception of control as responsiveness to individuals, not an
appreciation of the legitimacy of tighter externally imposed constraints. None of these people, nor any of their
colleagues, suggested that his or her behavior was significantly changed by interactions with citizens; mostly they
just gave answers or heard people out. But because they

did give answers and did hear people out, these bureaucrats did not think of themselves as isolated, untouchable figures. The problem of democratic control, therefore, is at least partly defused by allowing for responsiveness to individuals.

If with one hand administrators strip the concept of control of much of its meaning, with the other they alter what is generally thought of as its democratic element. Far from accepting democratically elected officials as legitimate agents of such control, the administrators I spoke with saw themselves as upholding democracy against the particularistic incursions of these officials. In bureaucratic eyes, mayors, board members, and members of the city council are not elected leaders of the citizenry, but rather politicians. And politicians are surely not the people to uphold democracy.

Many scholars have found that bureaucrats often have little use for politicians. They see them as privatistic, concerned only with their own electoral welfare or the interests of a narrow constituency. They are judged to be shortsighted, to believe that ends justify means, and generally to compare unfavorably with the bureaucrats themselves, who apply the same standards to all citizens in pursuit of the public interest. Discussing the French administrative elite, Ezra Suleiman explains, "For the Directors, a minister is first and foremost a politician. This means that his interests are always segmental, whether they concern the interests of his party, his local constituency, or even, for that matter, his ministry. They are never the general interest. The Directors see themselves, on the other hand, as the guardians of the general interest."[26] Robert Putnam writes of the "classical bureaucrat" who "distrusts or rejects the institutions of politics, such as par-

---

26. Suleiman, *Politics, Power and Bureaucracy*, p. 232.

liaments, parties, and pressure groups. To the classical bureaucrat, the noisy, incompetent, partisan practices of politicians seem at best senseless, at worst positively inimical to the permanent interests of the state."[27]

The bureaucrats I spoke with forcefully joined their voices to those quoted by other scholars. One educational administrator made his views known quite succinctly: "Politicians I abhor. I've seen many of them give half truths in order to accomplish their causes and without any thought or care evidently to what happens in the end." A colleague concurred: "Political groups gain power based on very short-term popular issues. Educational decisions affect a long period of time. It's much easier for the local political structure to do something that people want at a given time because it makes them popular for the next election." And still another colleague, discussing the mayor, maintained that "the mayor should be the farthest away from education. While he ought to be a member of the board, I don't think he should have a vote. He should be apprised on a monthly basis. That would give him the feedback and at the same time keep him away from education. . . . Once the mayor gets involved in education, then it becomes a political thing. And once it becomes a political thing, there's no end to it."

Lest one think that there is something peculiar about education operating here, listen to a housing administrator talk about political leaders:

> I've seen firsthand some of the incredibly bad things which have happened at this authority as a result of boards that are not interested in the authority but are only interested in serv-

---

27. Robert D. Putnam, "The Political Attitudes of Senior Civil Servants in Western Europe: A Preliminary Report," *British Journal of Political Science* 3 (July 1973): 259. Aberbach, Putnam, and Rockman similarly describe bureaucrats who "are dismayed by what they see as the chaotic collision of selfish interests, obscuring and subverting the commonweal" (*Bureaucrats and Politicians*, p. 149).

ing some alien political interest in the mayor's office. . . . Most boards, even so-called good boards, are normally going to be somewhat responsive to the appointing authority, and the appointing authority is political by nature. I suppose that has the potential to present problems, and if there was any way to restructure that, I would.

A colleague's comments suggest that from the bureaucrat's point of view, the problem lies not merely with local political leaders but with national ones as well. "Politics enters into things more often than it ought to. . . . Not that I think I'm an oracle of Delphi and can perceive everybody's best interest, but I can perceive it better than Congress can. And they're only interested in it from a political standpoint." And a fire administrator perhaps summed up the feelings of many when, discussing politicians, he concluded, "Thank God they leave us alone."

With such an opinion of political leaders, it is small wonder that democratic control by elected officials makes little sense to bureaucrats. Although no one said so in so many words, it was clear that to these people such control was tantamount to asking the fox to guard the chicken coop.[28] If anything, they see their role as guarding the public weal against the designs of politicians, and not as achieving it through those designs. Bureaucrats deny elected officials the right of control and deny it on the grounds that they are unfit governors, incapable of discerning the public interest. That is a task better left to the

---

28. Some might think that local officials, the heirs of Tammany Hall, are particularly likely to bring such perceptions on themselves. Federal officials, however, have proven themselves extremely capable of particularistic action as well. Morris P. Fiorina even entitles one section of his book on Congress "Tammany Hall Goes to Washington" (Fiorina, *Congress—Keystone of the Washington Establishment* [New Haven: Yale University Press, 1977]. Douglas Arnold also provides evidence of such particularism in congressional behavior (Arnold, *Congress and the Bureaucracy* [New Haven: Yale University Press, 1979], chaps. 6–8).

experts. Since it justifies a large measure of autonomy in bureaucratic eyes, this position can, of course, be self-serving. But political leaders also bring this on themselves. Every time a mayoral aide or a city council member calls a bureaucrat about a constituent problem, he or she reinforces the idea that the concerns of political leaders center on petty issues.[29]

By thinking about control as a greatly attenuated policy-making function or as minimal bureaucratic receptivity to individual citizens' complaints, bureaucrats are able to make their own jobs compatible with their broad democratic beliefs. By rejecting elected officials as pursuers of the public interest, bureaucrats are able to justify their rejection of interference by such officials and still be consistent in their belief in democracy. But what of the citizens themselves, the other potential agents of democratic control? How do the bureaucrats align their reluctance to admit control by the citizenry with their belief in democracy? The answer lies in a final sleight of thought that creates an exemption from democratic strictures for the specific agency involved. This enables the bureaucrats to accept democratic norms but deny their applicability to their own circumstances.

As I noted earlier, bureaucrats are somewhat more willing to grant the right of access (if not control) to citizens than to elected officials. Unfortunately, the citizens bureaucrats actually run into are often disappointing; they do little to suggest that they are truly capable of govern-

---

29. Suleiman reports a similar concentration on particularistic dealings in deputy-director interactions in France, with similar results for bureaucratic attitudes. He found that 75 percent of the civil servants questioned believed that the deputy "was not concerned with questions of general policy but only with making demands on behalf of his constituents" (*Politics, Power and Bureaucracy*, p. 291).

ing.[30] This sentiment was captured by an administrator in the housing authority who complained that "the reality that I have become accustomed with is [that] people who might otherwise have valid opinions, don't." Talking about the role the public should play in his agency, a fire administrator explained, "We're answerable to everybody if they have a legitimate reason. Mostly though it's personal gripes, something for personal gain. They don't come in and talk about their fellow citizens." And, when it is not personal gripes, bureaucrats often associate citizens' demands with the controversial issues of the day. At the time I was interviewing, affirmative action in hiring was such an issue, and the word "democracy" would recurrently set a respondent off on what were often tirades against affirmative action. Identified as the stalking horse for special interests, democracy itself thus loses its strength.

As a result of this dim view of citizens' behavior, many bureaucrats conclude that at times they must safeguard the public interest not only against the demands of politicians but also against parts of the public itself because of flaws in the public's ability to discern what is best. Talking about community groups, a school administrator told me that "because of pressure you have to respond in a different way [from the way you think is best] and possibly the way the public feels. And of course you do that but sacrifice the whole for the part." A colleague was less willing to make the sacrifice. In discussing the role of the public, he argued, "You listen to a problem, but when it comes time to make a decision, [you] make it on a hell of

30. Lipsky argues that street-level bureaucrats "mentally discount their clientele so as to reduce the tension resulting from their inability to deal with citizens according to ideal service models" (Lipsky, *Street-Level Bureaucracy*, pp. 140–41).

a lot more factors than what is politically popular at the moment."

In bureaucrats' eyes, popular ability to govern is also tempered by structural barriers posed by the complexity of their specific policy areas. Even if citizens were not behaving in a privatistic fashion, it would be difficult for them to comprehend fire, education, or housing policy. Three-quarters of my respondents maintained that the average citizen did not understand the work of their agencies; only four unreservedly thought the average citizen did.[31]

Assertions and data such as these might lead one to question whether bureaucrats really believe that people should govern themselves at all. Yet in spite of this skepticism about the motives of the public, these bureaucrats had a striking faith in people. "In general, do you think people know what is best for themselves?" I asked them, and only four said no. Fifteen gave an unqualified yes, while the rest hedged on a basically affirmative answer. The problem lies not with the general belief, but with its applicability to the particular circumstances confronting the specific bureaucrat. When asked about their own policy area (education, fire, or housing) the pattern of bureaucratic opinion about citizens' ability to make decisions was a mirror image of that for the general question. Thirteen said no, people did not know what was best for themselves; only three said yes; and the rest said, "Yes, but. . . ." As one administrator told me with perhaps surprising candor, "Oftentimes I think bureaucrats start be-

31. Others, too, have found that the reservations of bureaucrats about citizen knowledge and understanding are major impediments to increasing democratic control of bureaucracy. See, for example, Dale Mann, "Democratic Theory and Public Participation in Educational Policy Decision Making," in Frederick M. Wirt, ed., *The Polity of the School* (Lexington MA: Lexington Books, 1975); Aberbach and Rockman, "Administrators' Beliefs"; and Aberbach, Putnam, and Rockman, *Bureaucrats and Politicians*, chap. 6.

lieving that they know better what is best for people than people know themselves." Normative beliefs rest on certain assumptions—in this case that people are sufficiently expert, experienced, informed and farsighted to determine their own interests. Most of these bureaucrats seem to accept the validity of these assumptions in enough cases to accept the norm, but their experience in their own work leads them to reject it for their agencies. These data indicate, however, that such reservations are seen as exceptions and not the rule. Thus, the democratic norm of the competent citizen is maintained; it is just not relevant to the bureaucrat's particular case.

Our excursion into the terrain of bureaucratic beliefs has yielded useful information about the prospects for democratic control, with some potential openings on the road to reform. The path of moral exhortation seems notably doomed to failure. My conversations with bureaucrats have convinced me that appeals for cooperation based on democratic norms are likely to be met with nods of agreement when the norms are stated and acts of disagreement when it comes to daily behavior on the job. For that reason, too, emphasis on educating bureaucrats or hiring people with different values is also likely to produce frustration. The values these bureaucrats have are fine; they are just not heeded.[32]

In many cases the bureaucratic explanations for why norms are not acted on are clearly self-serving. By impugning the motives of elected officials and of ordinary

32. Lipsky argues that "popular wisdom often identifies the source of workers' attitudes toward clients and their jobs in prejudices acquired in upbringing and social background. Such perspectives lead to recommendations to hire better educated personnel or provide further education and training in public and human relations. All too often such perspectives fail to take account of the influence of street-level bureaucrats' work on their attitudes" (Lipsky, *Street-Level Bureaucracy*, p. 141).

citizens, the bureaucrats justify their own relative autonomy. Yet it would be a mistake to discount totally these explanations in thinking about reform. Self-serving or not, what bureaucrats believe shapes what bureaucrats do in response to control efforts.

Seeing the world through the bureaucrats' eyes also gives us a window through which to view how well the normative assumptions underlying various forms of control are, in fact, realized. In this way, bureaucratic attitudes mark perils on certain paths of reform. To the extent that bureaucrats are correct that the concerns of elected officials gravitate toward their own political gain, these beliefs signal a problem with increasing mayoral or council control over bureaucracy.[33] Similarly, to the extent that the bureaucrats are right about citizens being equally shortsighted, control by citizens that assumes that citizens will promote the collective interest is likely to go awry.

Finally, an understanding of the ways bureaucrats' daily lives affect the way they perceive the issue of democratic control suggests new ways of thinking about achieving that control. If one difficulty in bringing about control lies in the nature of the interactions bureaucrats have with the outside world, then one avenue for change may lie in changing those interactions. But to understand fully how this might be done, we first need to explore the ways in which bureaucracies, and hence the daily lives of bureaucrats, vary.

33. Heclo warns of the federal bureaucracy that "there are greater dangers in any reform that concentrates exclusively on responsiveness to political leadership. Without a sense of the civil services' independent responsibility to uphold legally constituted institutions and procedures, political control of the bureaucracy can easily go too far. Any single-minded commitment to executive energy is likely to evolve into arbitrary power" (Heclo, *Government of Strangers*, p. 244).

5

POLICY AREA AND
THE PROBLEM OF
DEMOCRATIC CONTROL

Inevitably, the complexities of policy making disturb the relative simplicity of our map of democratic control. To many people all bureaucrats may seem maddeningly alike, but the policy areas they work in surely are not. In the preceding chapters I examined the universal elements of the problems of achieving democratic control of bureaucracy. In this chapter and the next I look at the significance of differences among policy areas.

Differences among policy areas extend well beyond the particular issues in health, education, or foreign policy. Policy areas provide significantly different contexts for bureaucratic action, and hence significantly different variants on the problem of democratic control. Hugh Heclo warns of

> the sort of political workman who will be out of touch with his bureaucratic materials. . . . Not recognizing the strengths and weaknesses of his different materials, he will treat bureaucrats as interchangeable elements that are supposed to coalesce into a uniform whole without a self interest of their own. And as the grand design inevitably crumbles under the strains of the Washington environment, the political crafts-

man will walk away and leave the smoking workshop behind, muttering no doubt that all bureaucrats are the same anyhow.[1]

Our map reveals the general structure of the problem of democratic control of bureaucracy, but it is not sensitive to variations among policy areas. As a result, an important element for evaluating the consequences of specific control strategies is missing. Questions about norms and costs suggested by the map may be answered generally (as they have been in the previous chapters), but also with reference to individual policy areas. Similarly, though there are commonalities in the work lives of bureaucrats that shape their attitudes toward the issue of democratic control, there are also differences among these attitudes rooted in differences in the policy areas the bureaucrats work in.[2] Without an appreciation of these differences, we risk being the sort of political workman Heclo warns against.

In this chapter I begin the analysis of policy area vari-

1. Hugh Heclo, *A Government of Strangers* (Washington DC: Brookings Institution, 1977), p. 153. Other discussions of interbureaucratic and interagency variation can be found in Peter M. Blau and W. Richard Scott, *Formal Organizations* (London: Routledge and Kegan Paul, 1963); Anthony Downs, *Inside Bureaucracy* (Boston: Little, Brown, 1967); Leonard Reissman, "A Study of Role Conceptions in Bureaucracy," *Social Forces* 27 (1949): 305–10; and Harold Wilensky, "The Professionalization of Everybody?" *American Journal of Sociology* 70 (1964): 137–58.

2. Others have stressed the role policy area variation plays in the success of control efforts. Robert K. Yin and Douglas Yates (*Street-Level Governments* [Lexington MA: Lexington Books, 1975]), argue for the importance of service areas in explaining differences in the outcomes of decentralization strategies. Martha Wagner Weinberg (*Managing the State* [Cambridge MA: MIT Press, 1977], p. 8) suggests that "the single most striking feature about public agencies is that they differ greatly in their susceptibility to gubernatorial control." Virginia Gray ("Accountability in Policy Process: An Alternative Perspective," in Scott Greer, Ronald D. Hedlund, and James L. Gibson, eds., *Accountability in Urban Society: Public Agencies Under Fire* [Beverly Hills CA: Sage Publications, 1978]), and Douglas Yates (*Bureaucratic Democracy* [Cambridge MA: Harvard University Press, 1982], chap. 5) also address this issue.

ation by adopting the perspective of the would-be controller. I first consider the way variation among policy areas affects the controller's normative assumptions underlying the choice of control strategy. Then I consider the way variation among policy areas affects the costs of imposing control. In chapter 6, I switch to the perspective of the bureaucrat and examine how the policy area a bureaucrat works in affects the way he or she thinks about the issue of democratic control.

I shall look at policy area variation by borrowing two concepts from organization theory: technology and environment.[3] Technology refers to the means employed by an organization to achieve its desired ends. Although the term may sound most familiar in the industrial realm, it may be extended broadly. As Lyman Porter et al. argue:

> Technology is a term that is applicable to all types and kinds of organizations, not just industrial or manufacturing. All organizations, whether production-oriented or service-oriented, are presumed to involve individuals in some sort of activities that result in the transformation of "things" (requests, raw materials, people, communications, symbols, etc.) coming in into things going out. The fact that some of these techniques and activities deal with less tangible objects in no

3. Policy areas vary in many ways, and others have suggested numerous typologies. Perhaps the most influential is that of Theodore J. Lowi ("American Business, Public Policy, Case Studies, and Political Theory," *World Politics* 16 [1964]: 677–715). With this, as with most typologies of policy areas, what seems most persuasive is that variation exists and has consequences, and not that the specific categories developed are correct. Perhaps this is because the right classification has not been discovered. More likely, however, it is due to the extent of variation among policies, which makes no single typology able to capture all essential differences. For a related argument about the complexity of developing typologies of policy areas, see George D. Greenberg et al., "Developing Public Policy Theory," *American Political Science Review* 71 (1977): 1532–43. My interest is not in creating a new typology but rather in looking for patterns of variation that will help us understand the complexities of democractic control.

sense obviates the necessity to consider the technology of the operations to deal with them.[4]

The means a school district uses to educate children or a fire department uses to prevent and fight fires thus constitutes its technology. Technology provides one way of analyzing the distinctive work situation of bureaucrats in a given agency.[5] Just as different industries use different technologies, so, too, do different public agencies. These technologies vary not only in their individual idiosyncrasies (teaching children and putting out fires involve different activities) but also in such factors as how certain people are of the means needed to produce a given end and the degree of specialized expertise needed to employ the technology.

Environment, like technology, is a concept used by organization theorists to characterize private firms that is increasingly being applied to the public sector as well.[6] It refers to those forces outside an organization that affect the organization's activity. In terms of the operation of

4. Lyman W. Porter, Edward E. Lawler III, and J. Richard Hackman, *Behavior in Organizations* (New York: McGraw-Hill, 1975), pp. 232–33. Among the most notable discussions of technology thus broadly construed is that of James D. Thompson in *Organizations in Action* (New York: McGraw-Hill, 1967). James D. Thompson and Arthur Tuden ("Strategies, Structures, and Processes of Organizational Decision," in *Comparative Studies in Administration* [Pittsburgh: University of Pittsburgh Administrative Science Center, 1959], pp. 195–216) discuss the consequences of the state of knowledge about cause/effect relations for organizational structure and decision making.

5. The relationship between an agency and its prevailing technology is not immutable, of course. An agency's technology is subject both to innovation (as happened, for example, when computer-based instruction was introduced into schools) and to alteration if the goals of the agency change (as occurred in penal systems with the shift in emphasis from retribution to rehabilitation). Yet at any time the prevailing technology of a policy area can be identified.

6. See, for example, Thompson, *Organizations in Action*, chap. 3. For a summary discussion of the impact of environment on organizational design see Porter et al., *Behavior in Organizations*, pp. 227–31. Since the relationship of a bureaucracy to other political actors can be seen as an important design component, many of my arguments parallel those raised by scholars concerned with organizational design.

public agencies, considering the environment of bureaucracies draws our attention to such things as the degree of public conflict over bureaucratic goals, the complexity of the client groups the bureaucrats must deal with, the stability of the needs of those clients, and the independence of the work of the agency from that of other agencies. Environmental factors may have technological impacts. An environment of highly variable client need, for example, may be a source of technological uncertainty. Analytically, however, the concepts are distinct and may be considered separately.[7]

Variations in the technologies and environments of policy areas can create differences in the probabilities that specific costs of constraint will arise. They can also change the would-be controller's beliefs about the normative issues in the map. Thus a consideration of the ways policy areas vary in their technologies and environments is important to the would-be controller's choice among competing control alternatives.

NORMATIVE ASSUMPTIONS: TECHNOLOGICAL AND ENVIRONMENTAL VARIATION

First, let us look at how policy area differences affect answers to the bureaucratic variant of the question, How capable are people of governing themselves? There are

7. As with technology, an organization's environment is somewhat manipulable. In the area of social security for the elderly, for example, the bureaucratic environment is one of low variability among clients. Previous policy choices dictate that citizens be treated roughly the same way. A policy change in the direction of more finely calibrating pensions to recipient need would alter the bureaucratic environment to one in which clients would be more highly differentiated for the purposes of the work of the agency. Such alterations of bureaucratic environment are not common, however, and at any given time policy makers are confronted with an identifiable environmental context.

at least four components to such an ability. Citizens must be able to understand the work of an agency, they must be willing to use that understanding, they must be able to use that understanding effectively, and it must be appropriate for them to use it. The extent to which each of these components is present may vary across policy areas owing to differences in the technology and environment.

Understanding is highly susceptible to variations in the specialization of a policy area's technology. The more specialized the work of an agency, the harder it is for outsiders to understand that work and the more difficult it is to gain competence to govern.[8] As a result, though a would-be controller might believe in most cases that people are capable of governing themselves, in the case of agencies with highly specialized technologies, such as NASA, that same person might assume the opposite. The would-be controller might there want to opt for control strategies lying toward the lower left-hand corner of the map, where the capacity for self-governance is presumed to be low.

Even in specialized policy areas, however, significant opportunities for self-governance may remain. Many decisions in these domains require technical expertise, but others do not. The choice of a grade school reader, for example, rests in part on specialized knowledge of how well the vocabulary corresponds to student skills, but also

8. Arthur Maass (*Muddy Waters* [Cambridge MA: Harvard University Press, 1951], pp. 3–4), for example, argues that one of the primary reasons that legislators grant discretion to administrators is to make use of their technical expertise. The greater this expertise is, the more sensible this form of discretion would seem. On a more theoretical note Robert A. Dahl ("On Removing Certain Impediments to Democracy in the United States," *Political Science Quarterly* 92 [Spring 1977]: 12) argues that "probably no one who believes that full procedural democracy is a relevant aspiration thinks that it must hold for all matters, including judgments on highly technical, judicial, and administrative matters of every kind."

on the values imparted by the stories—a choice, many would argue, citizens can understand.[9] Furthermore, some scholars believe that no one knows the best way to teach children to read.[10] If that is the case, then even the seemingly technical aspects of the reader decision may be made on the basis of opinion and not of specialized knowledge, and thus be accessible to outside understanding.[11] Giandomenico Majone argues that even in highly complex policy areas such as environmental protection the scientific evidence on a policy question is often ambiguous, and that final decisions cannot be made according to traditional scientific criteria. For example, since there is disagreement over the level of exposure to carcinogens necessary to produce cancer in humans, decisions about safety standards often come down to decisions about how cautious one wishes to be.[12] Thus, variation across policy areas in technological complexity is important for an evaluation of popular ability, but so are differences among issues within a given policy area.

Citizen ability to understand the work of an agency is also affected by the visibility of a policy area's technology. In policy areas with highly visible technologies, the public can easily see and evaluate bureaucratic actions. A quick

9. See L. Harmon Zeigler and M. Kent Jennings, *Governing American Schools: Political Interaction in Local School Districts* (North Scituate MA: Duxbury, 1974), p. 248, for this argument.

10. Jeanne Chall, *Learning to Read: The Great Debate* (New York: McGraw-Hill, 1967).

11. Similarly, Dale Mann argues that it is unfair to bar citizens from decision making because their information levels do not live up to those required by a "rational" model of decision making, when there is evidence that administrators do not meet the demands of that model either (Mann, "Democratic Theory and Public Participation in Educational Policy Decision Making," in Frederick M. Wirt, ed., *The Polity of the School* [Lexington MA: Lexington Books, 1975], pp. 14–15).

12. Giandomenico Majone, "Process and Outcome in Regulatory Decisionmaking," *American Behavioral Scientist* 22 (1979): 561–83.

look down the streets, for example, will tell whether the garbage has been picked up.[13] Defense policy, on the other hand, is more distant; and its impact is apparent only under extreme circumstances, such as an embassy seizure or, worse, a war. It is therefore harder for the public to make judgments about the quality of work in defense-related organizations than in more visible policy areas. Without the power to judge the work of an agency, the ability that tightly constraining control mechanisms assume exists is difficult to acquire.[14]

Tightly constraining control mechanisms are also premised on the assumptions that citizens and/or their elected officials are willing and able to use their capacity to govern.[15] If citizens or elected officials are either unwilling to act or are prevented from acting, the control mechanism will misfire. In the first case control may formally exist, but the bureaucrats will in fact be free to act as they wish. Participatory structures that fail to attract widespread participation are an example. In the second case the operation of the control mechanism will be dis-

13. "In some cases the citizen can conduct his own program assessment. A recent national survey for the U.S. Senate found that the only government worker to get high marks from the public was the local trash collector, because at least people knew whether he was doing his job or not," Gray reports ("Accountability in Policy Process," p. 171).
14. "When we move still farther away from the private concerns of the family and the business office into those regions of national and international affairs that lack a direct and unmistakable link with those private concerns, individual volition, command of facts and method of inference soon cease to fulfill the requirements of the classical doctrine of democracy," Joseph A. Schumpeter argues (*Capitalism, Socialism and Democracy* [New York: Harper and Row, 1962], p. 260).
15. "Responsive systems require something from the public as well as from the elites, the government. Men must be able to translate their frustrations into articulate grievances and their grievances into effective demands. And they must see that their demands are placed before the right authorities in the right (most effective) way, and they must watch to see that something is done about it," Robert E. Lane writes (*Political Ideology* [New York: Free Press, 1962], p. 454).

torted because it will be used selectively by certain interests, as happens when participatory mechanisms come to be dominated by local elites.[16] The likelihood of either of these occurrences is affected, however, by environmental and technological variation across policy areas.

Conscious preferences in a policy area encourage people to turn latent competence for governance into political action.[17] Citizens are not, however, equally likely to have such preferences about all policy areas. Variation is partly caused by differences among agency technologies. It is hard to have preferences about the policies an agency pursues if you do not understand its work. Anthony Downs argues that "technical complexity may give [a bureau] relatively great freedom from external pressure" and that "the harder it is to perceive [a bureau's] success, the less a bureau is likely to receive clear signals about what it ought to do from the agents in its power setting."[18]

But technological variation alone does not explain variation across policy areas in the extent to which citizens express preferences; an environmental variable, the intensity of citizen preferences, also plays a role. Some policy areas are more important to citizens. Education, for example, is a policy area parents care deeply about, have opinions about, and express opinions about.[19] The activ-

16. An excellent example of such an occurrence can be found in Philip Selznick, *TVA and the Grass Roots* (New York: Harper and Row, 1966).

17. Note that this discussion is *not* about why some kinds of people participate and others do not. That question is amply addressed in works on political participation such as Sidney Verba and Norman Nie, *Participation in America* (New York: Harper and Row, 1972). Rather, my concern is about how differences among policy areas affect the likelihood that people will participate.

18. Downs, *Inside Bureaucracy*, pp. 209–10. Weinberg suggests that one of the reasons one of the agencies she studied was insulated from outside control was the complexity of its task (*Managing the State*, pp. 223–24).

19. There may be an obstacle to the ability of elected officials to govern if citizens have intensely held, but conflicting, preferences. Under those circumstances elected officials are faced with constituents who care deeply, but who as

ities of a parks department, on the other hand, occupy at most a peripheral corner in the lives of most citizens (and of most legislators). Even though those activities might be reasonably simple to understand and easy to evaluate, few citizens are likely to care enough to do anything about what the department does. Under such circumstances one might want to be cautious about adopting control mechanisms that assume a high degree of citizen ability not because citizens are not capable but because they are not likely to use their ability.

Another environmental variable, the density and distribution of organized groups in the population, may limit the ability of citizens to act. Where some preferences are represented by well-organized groups, but others are not, the unorganized may find it difficult to express their preferences effectively. In the area of agriculture, for example, those who produce the food may be much better able to govern themselves than those who consume it, not because the latter are untutored in agricultural technology but because their voices are so dispersed. James Q. Wilson argues that the distribution of organized activity within a policy area is determined by the distribution of costs and benefits of the policies involved. If either are concentrated, those who bear the costs or benefits are likely to organize.[20] In the example just given, the benefits of policies such as price supports are concentrated, whereas the costs are dispersed; hence farmers are well organized but shoppers are not. Under such circumstances one might hesitate before resorting to one of the clien-

a group give no clear guidance about what the official should do. Weinberg describes such a situation facing the governor of Massachusetts (*Managing the State*, p. 108).

20. James Q. Wilson, *Political Organizations* (New York: Basic Books, 1973), pp. 331–35. Also see Douglas Yates, *The Ungovernable City* (Cambridge MA: MIT Press, 1977), pp. 86–90, on this point.

tele-oriented strategies lying toward the center of the map, since such a control strategy would almost inevitably favor the organized.[21] Instead, entrusting control to a political actor able to see beyond the clamor of organized preferences might counteract this environmental impact.

Appropriateness of action is a final component of citizen competence. The technology of some policy areas almost dictates the deliberate exclusion of some actors from control processes. Regulatory and other agencies intended to control behavior are probably the best examples. Criminals may be quite capable of understanding the work of a corrections department, but it is the rare individual who advocates control over corrections by criminals. Similarly, employers may understand the work of the Equal Employment Opportunity Commission, but the purpose of that agency is to regulate, not be governed by, those affected interests. The deliberate exclusion of certain actors does not mean that such agencies must be free of control, but merely that clientele-oriented strategies that presume a wide distribution of competence are inappropriate.

The environment of other policy areas dictates that certain actors be favored rather than excluded. Some agencies, such as aging services and the Veterans Administration, work for limited and clearly identifiable client groups.[22] Though such clients may not be the only source

21. Another response, of course, might be to try to change this power imbalance. This strategy is discussed below in the concluding chapter.
22. Peter M. Blau and W. Richard Scott make this distinction between service and commonweal organizations. They warn of the danger of service organizations "considering it more important to protect the taxpayer than to serve clients adequately." They also warn, however, against giving clients too much control, since according to their definition a service agency is one in which the clients do not know what is best for themselves (Blau and Scott, *Formal Organizations* [London: Routledge and Kegan Paul, 1963], pp. 42–43, 52).

of control, would-be controllers may see them as especially competent, and hence a preferred set of actors.

A somewhat different approach to the issue of competence is to ask whether citizens possess pertinent information that bureaucrats do not themselves have. To the extent that citizens have such information, the assumption that they are capable of governing themselves is strengthened.[23] Such a conclusion would lead one to opt for more highly constraining control strategies. The extent to which citizens have special competence is a function of technological and environmental differences among policy areas.

One thing citizens might know is where the proverbial shoe pinches.[24] Although the proverb alleges that only the wearer knows this, in some domains feet have become so uniform that others can tell as well. In those areas bureaucrats know as well as citizens where the shoes, or their policies, pinch. But where the proverbial situation holds, citizens have a unique vantage point from which to judge an agency's work.[25]

Citizens are more likely to have such a vantage point in

23. Somewhat analogously, Victor Vroom and Philip Yetton argue that managers use more participatory decision processes when they do not possess all the necessary information for a high quality decision (Vroom and Yetton, *Leadership and Decision Making* [Pittsburgh: University of Pittsburgh Press, 1973], pp. 107–14).

24. "It is sadly instructive to find what a gap there always is between the account even the best administrations give of the effect of their regulations and the account you get from those to whom the regulations apply. The official account tells what ought to happen if men and women behaved and felt as decent respectable officials assume that they think and feel. What is actually happening is often quite different," writes A. D. Lindsay (*The Modern Democratic State* [New York: Oxford University Press, 1962], p. 270).

25. How great that measure actually is, is determined by the interaction of variability of need with the other factors affecting popular ability. When combined with a reasonably simple technology, for example, highly variable need should produce significantly greater ability than it would when combined with a specialized technology.

complex policy environments. A complex environment is one where client needs or demands are highly variable.[26] In the area of community development, for example, the needs and preferences of citizens change substantially from neighborhood to neighborhood. Bureaucrats would have a hard time knowing what those needs are without input from the residents. In the area of water quality, on the other hand, needs are much more uniform. Bureaucrats do not have to maintain close contact with citizens to find out if the water is clean enough for them—all they have to do is test the water.

A second kind of information that citizens have and bureaucrats need is what citizens are willing to do, or how they are willing to cooperate.[27] Agencies need cooperation when they do not command all the resources necessary for the success of their technology.[28] Sometimes this cooperation takes the form of compliance, sometimes the form of an active contribution of effort or knowledge. All technologies are not, however, equally reliant on cooperation.[29] For some agencies, such as the National

26. Yates discusses the importance of this variable, along with several other policy attributes, for urban policy making (*Ungovernable City*, especially chaps. 2 and 4).

27. This argument, too, is raised both by organization theorists and democratic theorists. Vroom and Yetton, for example, argue that need for acceptance is one variable determining whether participative decision making will occur (*Leadership and Decision Making*, p. 108). Lindsay argues that in addition to knowing where the shoe pinches, ordinary people know which policies they are willing to follow, and that this is a qualification for voting (*Modern Democratic State*, p. 269).

28. Jeffrey Pfeffer and Gerald R. Salancik (*The External Control of Organizations* [New York: Harper and Row, 1978], pp. 258–62) discuss the role of resource dependence in promoting interorganizational exchange and cooperation.

29. John D. Montgomery makes an analogous argument in his discussion of when participation is helpful to program administration. He argues that there are sensitivity areas "where local participation contributes to effective decision making". Among those sensitivity areas are "decisions that rest on information that varies from one district to another" and decisions that "demand

Weather Service, little cooperation is needed because all elements of the technology are contained within the agency itself. Schools, on the other hand, require significant cooperation from parents—supervising homework, getting the children to school on time, and so forth—in order to do their job of teaching children effectively. In this case important elements of the education technology are not controlled by the educators themselves. In policy areas where cooperation is important, citizens control an element vital to technological success. Since they understand an element of the agency's technology better than the bureaucrats, such control in turn grants citizens a measure of ability. How much ability it grants them depends on how vital the element in question actually is. In policy areas where cooperation is essential, the assumption of citizen ability that lies behind tighter forms of constraint is stronger.

Within the group of policy areas where cooperation is important lies a second source of variation: dispersion of control over absent resources. In the case of schools, this dispersion is quite great. At minimum all parents have some control over resources the schools need in the shape of information about what they are willing to do that is relevant to bureaucrats. By contrast, NASA is an example of an institution where there are needed resources beyond the control of the agency (technical expertise from the broader scientific community) but these resources are controlled by a very limited group of people. Taken together, these two variables suggest that the greater the resources outside the control of an agency *and* the greater the dispersion of that control, the stronger the support for the assumption of widespread citizen competence.

---

local changes in delivery or rationing systems." These categories roughly parallel shoe pinching and cooperation (Montgomery, "When Local Participation Helps," *Journal of Policy Analysis and Management* 3 [1983]: 94).

The second set of normative assumptions expressed in our map are two contrasting ideas about the role of democratic government. In chapter 2 I argued that the idea that the hallmark of democratic government is the preservation of the liberty of the citizenry is associated with control strategies near the procedural axis of the map, whereas the idea that democratic government exists to serve popular ends is implicit in control strategies lying near the substantive axis. One basis for choice of a control strategy is thus the would-be controller's assumptions about the goals of democratic government. This, too, may be conditional on the policy area at stake.

In some policy areas freedom from government action is more likely to be emphasized. Some technologies are focused on the provision of services, others on the regulation of behavior. When bureaucracies regulate behavior, people are being told what they may not do. Liberty is directly at stake.[30] Under such circumstances, even someone who naturally looks to government as an activist force is likely to express a concern for liberty and hence an interest in constraining bureaucratic procedures.[31]

Freedom from arbitrary government action may also be preferred in a bureaucratic environment where there is significant conflict over goals. Some conflict over goals is almost inevitable, but on some issues, such as fire, there is fairly widespread consensus about desired outcomes:

30. At the end of his article "Operative Doctrines of Representation" (*American Political Science Review* 62 [September, 1963]: 617), Charles E. Gilbert suggests that different traditions might be relevant to different policy areas. He suggests that several of the variables discussed here are important in this regard, including the extent to which a traditional "right" is at issue.

31. Jerry L. Mashaw writes about a related problem: whether bureaucratic systems should be designed to minimize false positives or false negatives. He argues that it is hard to determine which is more costly, but that among the ways to "make some headway" is to ask "whether the system is one that has a strong preference for one type of error against the other" (Mashaw, *Bureaucratic Justice* [New Haven: Yale University Press, 1983], pp. 84–85).

the fire department should save lives and protect property from fire damage. In the case of others, such as antipoverty programs, disagreement is the norm. Some segments of the population seek equalization of income, some seek to raise the income floor under the poor, some seek social and community development and others seek to trim the welfare rolls. In situations of conflict, it is harder to take the position that democratic government should serve public purposes, since these purposes are distinctly clouded. When there is no consensus about what goal should be pursued, procedure may loom more important to ensure that no party is grievously injured.[32]

The goal of liberty may also be paramount in policy areas with highly uncertain technologies. Certainty refers to how well the relationship of means to ends is known. For some government activities, cause-and-effect relationships are quite well known; in others they are not. Variation in the certainty of technology means that in some agencies, such as where government is involved in what is essentially a manufacturing process (generating electricity, paving streets, collecting garbage), bureaucrats can confidently be expected to achieve desired results; in other agencies, particularly those dealing with social policy, they cannot. Where we lack confidence in our ability to achieve a collective end, would-be controllers may consider safeguards against harmful government action to be particularly important. As Jerry Mashaw argues, "Where accuracy is impossible, or at least not demonstrable, the

32. Joseph Tussman (*Obligation and the Body Politic* [New York: Oxford University Press, 1974], pp. 71–72) argues that a fairness criterion for procedures comes into play in the face of disagreement over interest or purpose. Similarly, John C. Calhoun maintains that liberty is more at peril in a heterogeneous community (Calhoun, *A Disquisition on Government* [Indianapolis: Bobbs-Merrill, 1953], pp. 13–14).

net social value of decisionmaking may turn critically on an assessment of 'process value' cost and benefits."[33]

THE COSTS OF CONSTRAINT: TECHNOLOGICAL AND ENVIRONMENTAL VARIATION

In chapter 3 I discussed two costs associated with the imposition of constraint on bureaucracies: the enforcement cost and the effectiveness cost. Enforcement costs derive from ambiguities about why a bureaucrat has not adhered to a constraint. They arise when it is impossible to determine whether a constraint has been willfully ignored or has not been fulfilled owing to factors beyond the bureaucrat's control, such as technological or resource limitations. If the latter is the case, the bureaucrat is not culpable, and the controller is likely to be reluctant to impose penalties or likely to create difficulties by their imposition. Enforcement costs are associated with control strategies lying along the substantive axis of the map because these controls are more likely to entail asking bureaucrats to do things we are uncertain how to do, and thus more likely to create circumstances where it is hard to tell why a bureaucrat has not adhered to a constraint.

A second cost, loss of organizational effectiveness, occurs when control limits bureaucratic behavior in ways detrimental to the achievement of agency goals. This is more likely to occur when controllers place tight constraints on bureaucrats. Thus effectiveness costs are associated with control strategies lying in the highly constraining regions of the map. The relationship between control strategies lying in different regions of the map

33. Mashaw, *Bureaucratic Justice*, p. 88.

and the incidence of costs is a probabilistic one. However, the probabilities are not constant across all policy areas. Technological and environmental variations intervene.

Technological Variation

Two major sources of technological variation shape the connection between constraint and cost: the certainty of the technology and its degree of specialization. The ability to know why something has not happened provides the key to the link between certainty of technology and enforcement costs. One reason enforcement costs arise is that even well-intentioned bureaucrats may be unable to produce a specified outcome owing to insufficient knowledge. That is much less likely to happen in policy areas with certain technologies, since the certainty of the technology makes violation of a constraint much harder to excuse.[34] The most responsive bureaucrat in the country could not be expected to eliminate unemployment among ghetto youth, because the technology is highly uncertain. Even the best experts in the country do not know how to do so. But if streets remain pocked with potholes after a legislative decision to allocate money for their repaving, a bureaucrat would be hard pressed to claim that he or she tried to comply with the legislative mandate, but just did not know how to do so. Under those circumstances substantive constraints that are normally prone to enforcement problems will be less costly. On the other hand, enforcement difficulties are more likely to arise in policy areas where technology is more uncertain.[35] In those pol-

34. "For some engineering fields program accountability is possible. Production may be shut down if a weapon does not perform as promised," Gray suggests ("Accountability in Policy Process," p. 170).

35. Yates argues that agencies are difficult to manage where technology is weak, because consistent and reliable operating procedures are absent (*Bureaucratic Democracy*, p. 131).

icy areas, reliance on substantive constraint may become, in effect, an abdication of any form of control; faced with an unattainable constraint, the bureaucrat may well decide to act purely as he or she sees fit. Under such circumstances procedural constraint or very weak outcome constraints—that is, those constraints less prone to incurring enforcement costs—emerge as more promising avenues of control.[36]

Certainty of technology also affects the likelihood that limited resources will produce enforcement problems. A certain technology means not only that we know how to do something but also that we can confidently estimate how much it will cost. Confidence in cost estimates, in turn, increases the likelihood of successful constraint in two ways. First, adequacy of resources is more easily determined, and hence claims of inadequate resources are easier to evaluate. It is relatively easy to determine what it costs to fill potholes. The claims of a highway administrator who explained the persistence of axle-threatening streets by claiming inadequate resources could easily be checked up on by examining his or her budget. On the other hand, an evaluation of similar claims from a manpower administrator with unemployed clients would be more difficult.

Second, where costs are relatively certain, the imposition of a constraint is more likely to be accompanied by an adequate allocation of resources, because a disjuncture between the constraint and the appropriation will be more immediately apparent. Congress is unlikely to tell

36. "If the correctness or fairness of the outcomes can be determined unambiguously the manner in which the decision is made is largely immaterial; only results count. But when the factual and value premises are moot, when no independent criterion for the right result exists, the process or procedure of decision making acquires special significance," Majone maintains ("Process and Outcome," pp. 577–78).

the Army Corps of Engineers to build a dam, but only provide enough money to build half of it (though it is not incapable of doing that). In contrast, we often tell parole officers to rehabilitate juvenile delinquents, but provide funds that may or may not be adequate to do the job, since we do not know how to rehabilitate juvenile delinquents and are unable to estimate what adequate funding would be in the first place. Thus, the more certain the technology, the more certain other political actors can be about whether resource limitations have intervened to impede bureaucratic compliance with a constraint. As a result, enforcement costs are less likely to arise in policy areas with certain technologies.

Technological variation also affects the susceptibility of policy areas to effectiveness costs from constraint. As I argued in chapter 3, constraint may produce effectiveness costs in two ways. Controllers may either tell bureaucrats to do the wrong thing—that is, to behave in a way that will not achieve desired goals—or they may unduly restrict bureaucratic flexibility regardless of the content of the constraint. Policy areas with highly specialized technologies are particularly susceptible to effectiveness costs stemming from the imposition of wrong constraints. In such policy areas (as, for example, nuclear energy or medicine) bureaucrats must possess specialized expertise in order to do their jobs. By definition this expertise is not commanded—and often not understood—by nonspecialists. Under such circumstances, efforts by outsiders to dictate precisely how bureaucrats should behave are likely to have adverse consequences on the work of the agency. In contrast, where the technology is simpler and easier for nonspecialists to understand, outsiders are more likely to be able to limit bureaucratic behavior closely without serious cost to effectiveness. Close congressional specification of how research and development funds should be spent is much more likely to result in ineffective deployment of those funds, for example, than is equally close specification of how food stamp money is to be allocated. In the research and development case, Congress is unlikely to be able to master the specialized knowledge needed to evaluate grant proposals, whereas in the food stamp case the technological issues should be much more comprehensible.

Policy areas with uncertain technologies are also particularly susceptible to effectiveness costs caused by undue constraint. Where exact means/ends relationships are not known (either because the technology is not fully developed or because it is one in which constant feedback is necessary in order to determine how to proceed),[37] greater latitude of administrative action may be necessary to produce desired results. In such policy areas performance gaps are more likely when latitude is denied.[38] The technology involved in police protection, for example, is much less certain than that involved in garbage collection. As a result, the deleterious effects of precisely specifying the time a patrolman should walk down a particular street are likely to be far greater than those of an equally precise specification of the time garbage is to be picked up on that street. In policy areas characterized by uncertain technologies, tight constraint can thus be particularly costly.

37. Thompson describes such technologies as intensive technologies and describes them in *Organizations in Action*, chap. 2.
38. Downs argues that "performance gaps" are more likely to be experienced by bureaus with innovation-prone as opposed to stable technologies (*Inside Bureaucracy*, p. 209). Thompson and Tuden suggest that where there is disagreement over beliefs about causation, decision strategies must allow for greater flexibility ("Organizational Decision," pp. 199–200). And Michael Lipsky argues that in service areas where flexibility is necessary, efforts to limit discretion in the interest of accountability are likely to have serious effects on the quality of service (Lipsky, "The Assault on Human Services: Street-Level Bureaucrats, Accountability, and the Fiscal Crisis," in Greer et al., eds., *Accountability*).

The potential for effectiveness costs is compounded in policy areas where technology is both uncertain and knowledge concerning the technology highly specialized. Under such circumstances tight constraint may create problems either by being wrong or by being excessive, or both. The field of nuclear safety increasingly seems to be an example of this. We have become painfully aware that we do not confidently know how to clean up nuclear accidents, yet what is known about such cleanups is highly specialized. Tight constraint of bureaucratic behavior in this policy area might therefore create effectiveness costs to the work of the agency either by depriving the bureaucrats of needed flexibility to experiment or by dictating the wrong experiments.

Environmental Variation

Bureaucrats operating in different policy areas not only work with different kinds of technologies, they also face different environments. Like technological variation, environmental variation has consequences for the likelihood that the enforcement and effectiveness costs associated with various forms of constraint will arise. Four characteristics of environments are particularly important in this regard: conflict, instability, complexity, and independence.

In policy areas characterized by conflict over goals, different political actors are likely to have significantly different expectations about bureaucratic performance and thus to seek to impose conflicting constraints. This in turn affects the susceptibility of control to enforcement costs; conflicting constraints can be used as a justification for noncompliance with any given constraint. The difficulty of imposing sanctions under such circumstances creates enforcement costs.[39] In those policy areas where an environment of goal conflict is the norm there is thus a greater probability that the enforcement costs associated with substantive constraint will actually be incurred; and would-be controllers may therefore prefer less susceptible procedural or substantive output constraints.

The early years of the Title I compensatory education program provide an excellent example. That program was passed by assembling an uneasy coalition of people interested in general aid for education and people interested in aid aimed at poor children. As a result, local school administrators received conflicting signals as to how Title I money should be spent, and federal officials found it very difficult to enforce several provisions of the law.[40] The history of Title I regulations is, in fact, marked by a movement toward constraints that are less susceptible to enforcement costs. In amendments to the original legislation, Congress imposed procedural constraints (such as the requirement that bureaucrats conduct needs assessments before designing Title I programs) and substantive constraints couched in output terms (such as the comparability requirement stipulating that local budgetary allocations may not discriminate between schools that

39. A number of authors have noted the relationship between goal ambiguity and difficulty of control in public agencies. Weinberg argues that the "clarity of the central task" of an agency is important in determining how controllable the agency is: "The clearer and the more limited the goals of any agency, the more obvious the criteria for evaluating a manager's performance will be" (*Managing the State*, p. 221). Similarly, Michael Lipsky suggests that lack of agreement about objectives makes an organization hard to evaluate (Lipsky, *Street-Level Bureaucracy* [New York: Russell Sage Foundation, 1980], p. 49). In the same vein Mashaw writes: "The more specific and objective the goals of the organization can be made, the easier it will be to determine whether or not performance meets expectations" (*Bureaucratic Justice*, p. 149). Yates argues that it is easier to control bureaucracies that have what he calls a "unified mission" (*Bureaucratic Democracy*, p. 127).

40. Jerome T. Murphy, "The Education Bureaucracies Implement Novel Policy: The Politics of Title I ESEA, 1965–1972," in Allan P. Sindler, ed., *Policy and Politics in America* (Boston: Little, Brown, 1973), pp. 160–98.

do and do not receive federal funds for compensatory education) on bureaucrats administering the Title I program.

An environment of goal conflict also increases the susceptibility of policy areas to effectiveness costs. Although conflicting constraints may at times be used by bureaucrats as an excuse to avoid constraint, attempts to obey conflicting constraints may hamper the work of the agency. The tighter those constraints are, of course, the more likely it is that this will happen, since tight constraints leave bureaucrats less room for maneuver.[41]

A second way environments vary is in the degree of their stability. An unstable bureaucratic environment occurs where the needs and/or demands of the public served shift over time; a stable environment exists where these needs are relatively constant. A school system serving a city whose population is undergoing significant demographic change has an unstable environment, for example, because it has to adjust rapidly to very different kinds of pupils, with very different educational needs. The water department in the same city, however, has a much more stable environment. It will be facing essentially the same patterns of demand as long as the size of the city remains fairly constant.[42]

Since there is inevitably a time lapse between the im-

41. Lipsky comes at this issue from the other direction by arguing that the clearer the goals for an agency are, "the more finely tuned guidance can be" (*Street Level Bureaucracy*, p. 40).
42. Environment and technology are not always neatly separable concepts. An unstable environment may, for example, be a cause of technological uncertainty. Yet the two concepts are not the same and it is analytically useful to consider them separately. Technological uncertainty may occur even in a highly stable environment, and environmental instability may occur even where technology is quite certain. The problem of the relationship between these two variables is discussed in P. Lawrence and J. Lorsch, *Organization and Environment* (Boston: Harvard Business School, 1967).

position of a constraint by a political actor and its actual impact on bureaucratic behavior, instability is important to the problem of democratic control. In an unstable environment the conditions confronting the political actor when the constraint is imposed may be significantly different from those that later confront the bureaucrat. Changing conditions in turn increase the likelihood that the constraint will be the wrong one, and therefore increase the probability that effectiveness costs will arise. For example, the quality of urban education would be more affected by confining curricula and teacher deployment decisions made a decade ago than the quality of urban water supply would be by comparably confining constraints. For policy areas where the environment is relatively stable, the incidence of effectiveness costs from tight constraint should therefore generally be lower than for those policy areas where instability is an important fact of bureaucratic life.[43]

A third source of environmental variation, complexity, may also affect the incidence of effectiveness costs. In simple policy environments, like garbage collection, the needs of all citizens are more or less the same; in complex ones, like mental health, they are highly variable. Bureaucrats operating in complex environments must be able to adjust their behavior continuously to the needs of the client at hand, and the pattern of such adjustments is

---

43. Downs maintains that "performance gaps appear more frequently and expand faster in bureaus dealing with rapidly changing external environments than in those dealing with relatively stable ones. Consequently, the former must be able to change their behavior quickly whereas the latter can concentrate their efforts upon performing existing tasks with maximum efficiency" (*Inside Bureaucracy*, p. 208). Similarly, organization theorists argue that tightly structured organizations are a liability in an unstable environment. See Porter et al., *Behavior in Organizations*, pp. 227–28, and Thompson, *Organizations in Action*, chap. 6.

hard to specify in advance.[44] Mental health personnel must be able to adapt their behavior to each client if their service is to be delivered effectively, whereas garbage collectors do not have to adjust to widely varying collection needs from house to house.

The need for flexibility created by a complex environment forges the link between this environmental attribute and the susceptibility of policy areas to effectiveness costs. Like an unstable environment, a complex one can create greater potential effectiveness problems if bureaucratic behavior is tightly constrained. Such constraint limits the flexibility a complex environment demands.[45] Where needs are more uniform or predictable, the costs of tight constraints to organizational effectiveness are likely to be much lower, because flexibility is less important.

A final environmental attribute that has consequences for the costs of constraint is agency autonomy. No agency can be completely immune to the actions of others, but bureaucrats find some policy areas reasonably self-contained: the problems they deal with are discrete, the impact of their actions on other bureaucrats is limited. State departments of motor vehicles, for example, by and large work alone. Other agencies are woven into a tight web of interdependence; issues are broader; ripple effects are greater (or, to use the economists' term, they both create and are subject to significant externalities). The work of

44. Lipsky describes "street-level bureaucrats" who "have discretion because the accepted definitions of their tasks call for sensitive observation and judgment, which are not reducible to programmed formats" (*Street Level Bureaucracy*, p. 15).

45. Lipsky in fact argues that accountability is virtually impossible in such an environment: "It is a contradiction in terms to say that the worker should be accountable to respond to each client in the unique fashion appropriate to the presenting case. For no accountability can exist if the agency does not know what response it prefers, and it cannot assert a preferred response if each worker should be open to the possibility that unique and fresh responses are appropriate" (*Street-Level Bureaucracy*, p. 162).

a city's housing agency, for example, is greatly affected by—and itself greatly affects—the work of the redevelopment agency, which is in turn affected by the city planning commission. Constraints imposed on any one will have ripple effects on the others. In an environment where independence is high, the constraints imposed on one agency are largely irrelevant to the work of others. Where interdependence is the norm, however, tight constraints on one may create effectiveness costs for others. Flexibility is necessary in order that a redevelopment agency may, for example, adjust its behavior to accord with what the planning commission is doing.[46] For policy areas where bureaucrats are operating in an interdependent environment, tight constraints are thus more likely to create serious effectiveness costs than they are for policy areas in environments of greater independence.

Taken as a whole, technological and environmental variations form a complex mosaic. The various policy dimensions come together in different ways for different agencies and often do not speak to the problem of democratic control with a united voice. For example, someone seeking to control a bureaucracy that faces an environment of variable client needs might want to consider both that this variability creates a need for flexibility for the agency, and hence potential effectiveness problems if tight constraint is imposed, and that clients have some important information for the agency, and hence should be allowed a measure of control. The technological and environmental characteristics of a policy area may also change as goal consensus builds or evaporates, or as technology becomes

46. Don K. Price, for example, argues that complex tasks call for decisions to be "made from a broader point of view than any single agency" (Price, *The Scientific Estate* [Cambridge MA: Harvard University Press, Belknap Press, 1965], p. 246).

more specialized or certain. Yet the specific needs of specific policy areas are important, and important in predictable ways. The problem of controlling bureaucracies crosses all agency boundaries; particular solutions often do not. An analysis of technology and environment provides a guide for the would-be controller's choice of control mechanism. It allows the controller systematically to consider the benefits and costs of applying control strategies in particular circumstances.

6

PERCEPTUAL FILTERS: A BUREAUCRAT'S-EYE VIEW OF OUTSIDE INTERVENTION

If all bureaucrats resisted all control at all times, public agencies would look more like battlefields than even caricaturists depict. Reality is better described in terms of skirmishes than as warfare. Bureaucrats have crafted substantial armor to defend themselves against outside efforts to constrain their behavior, but that armor does have chinks in it through which some democratic control may pass. The analyst who wishes to understand bureaucratic control and the policymaker who wishes to design ways of achieving it must therefore take the measure of the chinks as well as of the armor.

As we have just seen, bureaucracies in different policy areas vary in their core technologies and in the environments in which they operate. These variations create different work situations for the bureaucrats and encourage different attitudinal patterns. Robert Lane argues, "The daily events of a person's work life, the pattern of his working associations, the responses and attitudes demanded by his job inevitably mold and shape his inventory of character traits. Men confronted by similar occupational events, associations, and demands will be

149

similarly influenced."[1] Attitudinal patterns may be fortified by others sharing the workplace. Peter Blau maintains that "the social values that prevail in a work group do exert external constraints on the thinking and acting of its members."[2] And Aaron Wildavsky argues that "as the members of the organization learn to interpret the world in fixed ways, they tend to perceive events to fit in with their existing frames of reference. To the extent that members share common simplifications about the world, they reinforce one another in the strength of their convictions."[3] Such shared convictions in turn have consequences for democratic control. In studies of federal bureaucrats Bob Wynia found that bureaucrats in different agencies had different patterns of democratic beliefs,[4] and Joel Aberbach and Bert Rockman found agency effects on attitudes about equity of representation.[5] These findings all suggest that further exploration of work-related attitudes should yield rich results in terms of understanding when bureaucrats accept certain forms of democratic control.

1. Robert E. Lane, *The Regulation of Businessmen* (Hamden CT: Archon Books, 1966), p. 72.

2. Peter M. Blau, "Structural Effects," in Peter M. Blau, *On the Nature of Organizations* (New York: John Wiley and Sons, 1974), p. 82.

3. Aaron Wildavsky, "The Analysis of Issue Contexts in the Study of Decision Making," *Journal of Politics* 24 (1962): 718. "Any form of organization, including bureaus, will differentially reward those whose capabilities and attitudes best serve the organization, and people will sort themselves out among forms of organization depending on their perceived reward," William A. Niskanen, Jr., further argues in *Bureaucracy and Representative Government* (Chicago: Aldine-Atherton, 1971), p. 23. My data cannot, however, distinguish between attitude patterns that are the result of recruitment and those that are the result of socialization.

4. Bob L. Wynia, "Federal Bureaucrats' Attitudes Toward a Democratic Ideology," *Public Administration Review* 34 (1974): 156–62.

5. Joel D. Aberbach and Bert A. Rockman, "Clashing Beliefs Within the Executive Branch: The Nixon Administration Bureaucracy," *American Political Science Review* 70 (1976): 456–68.

I argue that the technological and environmental attributes of the jobs of bureaucrats working in different policy areas mold bureaucratic attitudes about work into characteristic patterns. These work-related attitudes create what may be thought of as perceptual filters through which bureaucrats view the outside world.[6] The correspondence between agency and filter is not perfect, of course; we would hardly expect it to be. Work-related attitudes derive from more sources than just the objective characteristics of the work place. Furthermore, some agency officials have jobs that deviate from agency norms. But, as we shall see, these aberrant cases frequently have aberrant belief patterns, thus reinforcing our confidence that job attributes and beliefs are related.

Filters can be powerful blocking mechanisms. One of the major functions perceptual filters serve is to make certain kinds of control appear particularly threatening and thus worthy of vigorous resistance, but the filter, and hence the offending control, varies. Different policy areas create quite different blocking filters. Filters also cause some forms of control to stand out as acceptable to the bureaucrat. Workplace variation creates two such types of perceptual filters: those that cause bureaucrats to perceive certain controls as legitimate and those that cause bureaucrats to perceive certain controls as useful.[7]

6. This argument is akin to Robert D. Putnam's contention that "the cognitive predispositions of political leaders function like perceptual sets, influencing, though seldom wholly determining, the ways in which issues are conceived and analyzed" (Putnam, *The Beliefs of Politicians* [New Haven: Yale University Press, 1973], p. 127).

7. Legitimacy and utility may be seen as loosely linked to two of Charles E. Lindblom's modes of social control: authority and exchange. The correspondence is only partial, however, since Lindblom argues that authority does not necessarily imply legitimacy, and since much of what I describe as utility consists of what Lindblom calls extended use of authority, or mutual adjustment (Lindblom, *Politics and Markets* [New York: Basic Books, 1977], especially chaps. 1–3).

CORE IDENTITIES: EXPERTS, WORKERS,
AND ADMINISTRATORS

Bureaucrats rarely think of themselves as public officials. Rather they think of themselves as people at work, and this mundane, but critical, identity profoundly affects bureaucratic responses to democratic control. My interviews reveal that administrators working in different policy areas have identifiable and distinct "core identities" that in turn create different patterns of resistance to democratic control. The work bureaucrats do varies significantly. Some of this variation occurs within agencies. In any bureaucracy there are people doing quite different jobs at different levels within the administrative hierarchy. Variation across policy areas is, however, of central importance for democratic control. Teachers and firemen do different kinds of things because education and fire fighting involve different kinds of technology. The work of administrators in different agencies reflects such technological differences, as does the way administrators think about their jobs.[8]

I define a bureaucrat's core identity as the way that bureaucrat thinks of himself or herself at work. I discerned these identities from the way the bureaucrats talked about their jobs. In the course of discussing the way bureaucrats

---

8. Others have suggested the importance of policy environment to bureaucratic attitudes. In the United States and Germany "a civil servant's ideological stance is much more closely related to the department in which he works than to his sociopolitical origins," Joel D. Aberbach, Robert D. Putnam, and Bert A. Rockman found in *Bureaucrats and Politicians in Western Democracies* (Cambridge MA: Harvard University Press, 1981), p. 162. Michael Lipsky, looking at the issue of implementation, argues that "one should focus on how the work is experienced by policy deliverers. One should concentrate on those pressures generated by the agency, such as rules and inducements, and those that prevail for other reasons" (Lipsky, "Standing the Study of Public Policy Implementation on Its Head," in Walter Dean Burnham and Martha Wagner Weinberg, eds., *American Politics and Public Policy* [Cambridge MA: MIT Press, 1978], p. 398).

saw their jobs, what they liked and disliked about them, what their goals were, what the obstacles to achieving those goals were, and what qualities the bureaucrats thought were important in a good administrator, three quite different identities were evident. There were the experts whose primary concerns revolved around the substance of their work, the workers whose primary concerns centered on the workplace itself, and the administrators whose primary concerns were the administrative tasks at hand. In each agency one of these identities predominated.

Since the core identity is a work identity, it is not surprising that the predominant identity of workers in an agency can be predicted from the dominant technology of the policy area. Different technologies create different kinds of demands on the job. These demands, in turn, both attract different kinds of people and reinforce the importance of certain kinds of skills. In policy areas where the dominant technology is specialized, bureaucrats must be highly trained. They are employed for their expertise and work in concert with others who share it. Such bureaucrats are likely to think of themselves as substantive experts. What attracts them to a job is the substance of the decisions being made. What fulfills them is their ability to apply their expertise to realize substantive goals.

Education is nowhere near the extreme of specialization, but its practitioners generally do consider themselves to be expert professionals. University schools of education certainly contribute to this, as do advanced degree requirements for high-level administrative positions.[9] The core identity of the education administrators

9. L. Harmon Zeigler and M. Kent Jennings (*Governing American Schools* [North Scituate MA: Duxbury, 1974], p. 140) describe superintendents as "professional vagabonds. They tend to be as much or more oriented to their

I spoke with revolves very much around the substance of education and their expertise in it. When asked why they came to work for the department of education, typical responses were, "I enjoy working with students," or, "I'd always wanted to be a teacher." Virtually all educational administrators start out as teachers, and perhaps not surprisingly all but two (of eighteen) I spoke with emphasized a substantive interest in working for the agency. Similarly, when asked what they liked most about their job, all but three answered by talking about the substance of their work—educating children[10] (as compared to only half[11] in housing and slightly fewer than half in fire whose answers were about providing housing or fighting fires). One education administrator, for example, said, "I think by and large the greatest reward for me comes from knowing that the entire operation is providing much-needed, appropriate services for children." Another answered, "The greatest rewards are seeing kids happy and learning."

A substantive focus also emerged in discussions of what these bureaucrats saw as the greatest obstacles to achieving their goals. The obstacles they raised most frequently were obstacles to learning: "Television. The kids watch so

---

profession as they are to their particular contemporary districts." The literature on professionalism is, of course, tremendous. Authors who discuss professional identification within a bureaucratic context include Harold Wilensky, "The Professionalization of Everybody?" *American Journal of Sociology* 70 (1964): 137–58; Leonard Reissman, "A Study of Role Conceptions in Bureaucracy," *Social Forces* 27 (1949): 305–10; and Frederick C. Mosher, *Democracy and the Public Service* (New York: Oxford University Press, 1968).

10. Reissman discusses the "functional bureaucrat . . . who is oriented towards and seeks recognition from a given professional group. . . . His evaluations of success and accomplishment are not measured in terms of satisfactorily fulfilling a given bureaucratic policy or aim . . . but rather in terms of the professional quality with which he does his job" ("A Study of Role Conceptions," p. 308).

11. Exact percentage figures for responses discussed in this chapter may be found in Appendix II.

much of it," or, "A lack of communication between teachers and parents," or "The environment of the home." Over half of the bureaucrats in education stressed such substantive problems, compared to only one in housing and two in fire who perceived their chief problems as housing or fire-fighting problems. Interestingly, when asked what they disliked about their jobs, the most common response of bureaucrats in the education department was to point to some aspect of their administrative duties. Clearly, these were educators first, bureaucrats second. As one described his idea of a good school administrator: "You really have to know what education's all about so that people really have a trust in you that you are an educator and you can make a difference in the lives of their children."

Fire fighting, in contrast, is a relatively unspecialized technology. Education requirements for employment are low, and skills are learned on the job. The core identity of fire administrators does not lie in their expertise, credentials, or substantive knowledge, but in their mastery of the workplace itself. They see themselves as workers, not as experts.[12] A clue to the organizational focus of fire administrators lies in their length of tenure within the department. All the fire administrators I spoke with had been with the agency over twenty years. The most common reason they gave for joining the fire department was the very pragmatic one of security: "You went through

12. Reissman similarly describes the "job bureaucrat. . . . He is immersed entirely within the structure. Professional skills only provide the necessary entrance qualifications and determine the nature of the work to be done. . . . His aspirations consist of achieving material rewards and increased status through promotions. He strongly adheres to the rules and the job constitutes his full center of attention and the end to be served" ("A Study of Role Conceptions," p. 309). Compare, too, with Alvin W. Gouldner's cosmopolitans and locals (Gouldner, "Cosmopolitans and Locals: Toward an Analysis of Latent Social Roles," *Administrative Science Quarterly* [1957]: 281–306).

part of the depression years, and you were looking for security"; "Well, I had a family then, a wife and children. . . . I thought that the security of the civil service job would be a good thing to have." Approximately half of the fire administrators mentioned such considerations, whereas no one in either the education or housing departments suggested security was a primary reason for taking their jobs.

Working conditions dominate fire administrators' discussions of what they like about their jobs: "It's a good job, it pays well. It's hard at times, but it's not hard all the time." And again the security theme: "Well, it provides security for my family. It's allowed me to educate my children and send all of them to college." And what do fire administrators dislike about their jobs? The biggest complaints were over the attitude of the people working for them and the size of their own salaries. Such workplace considerations accounted for about half of the answers from fire administrators, as against less than a third from housing and education. Similarly, when fire administrators were asked how they would compare their job to one in the private sector, about half answered in terms of the nature of the working conditions (compared to under a quarter in housing and education): "It would be much different as far as the financial gains of it"; "I have much more freedom here." Finally, when asked to describe a good fire administrator, over half emphasized the ability to work well with the staff. This suggests a quite different orientation from that of the education administrators, among whom over half stressed the need for substantive expertise.

Housing bureaucrats live in yet a third world. Their jobs do not entail manipulation of a single dominant technology but rather the coordination of many. Housing administrators spend their days planning, building, managing, financing, and maintaining public housing. Their contribution lies not in doing any single aspect of this, but in making sure that all elements of the public housing program work together and work in a way congruent with myriad state and federal mandates. As a result, they are quintessential administrators. As one described her job, "Very nutsy boltsy, if I can put it that way. I enjoy little minutia kinds of work, and getting things right. So I don't have any great fantasies about doing great things for poor people. I'm a wheel greaser."

Housing administrators are itinerants who are not tied to a single policy area. Over half of those I spoke with had worked for the agency for less than five years, and almost half said they expected to be out of housing and into some other field of public sector administration in five years. This was the only agency in which respondents saw themselves moving into other areas of public administration. When asked why they came to work for the housing authority, the bureaucrats I spoke with gave answers that clearly suggested their administrative orientation: "I was more interested in getting further into the social service field and getting away from public housing . . . but when the job possibility presented itself I weighed the pros and cons and it was a very good opportunity. . . . I guess basically five years from now I see myself out of the public housing field and just into public service in some way." Similarly, another bureaucrat replied, "The one gap in my experience at that time was housing so I thought it was a real natural."

As in education and fire, the core identity of housing administrators is vividly revealed in their discussions of their jobs. As one would expect of administrators, they enjoy getting things done. One described the rewards of her job as "getting things to work right . . . getting all the project offices to do something right or to do it the same way at least. Getting it to function smoothly." Almost half of the housing administrators answered that what they liked most about their job was the sense of accomplishment in problem solving it provided (as opposed to only one in fire, and none in education). Equally, what they do not like about their jobs are things that impede getting things done: "Well, there are some problems here with staff, with people filling positions that they are not necessarily suited for but they've sort of grown into. That makes the organization sometimes run in a very unwieldy fashion and not a very effective way." Others stressed restrictions on their flexibility and financial limitations as things they did not like about their jobs. The obstacles they saw to achieving their goals were much the same: "Money in the first instance and then the limitations of bureaucracy in the second. In anything that you want to do, you end up either with these red tape kind of procedures that stand in your way and make the time element impossible or perhaps even a bigger frustration is running into incompetence where you need ability."

Bureaucrats in the housing authority also showed their administrative colors when talking about what they looked for in a good housing administrator. Educators stressed substantive knowledge; fire officials relied on leadership ability. In housing the keys are managerial qualities such as administrative skills and the capacity to assume responsibility or make decisions: "I'm more of a believer in the generalist type of administrator, not one that has gone to housing school if there was such a school. As long as you've got brains and some imagination and some sort of measure of ability, you can learn some of the details or have people working for you who know some of the details." More simply, another said she would look for "a questioning, inquisitive individual." Then she added, "That is almost what a good anything is."

Three individuals exemplify these three core identities—the expert, the worker, and the administrator.[13] John Cavaliere is an expert educator with a B.A., M.A., and Ph.D. in educational administration. He joined the school system on leaving college and when I interviewed him had been with it for twelve years, first as a teacher, then a principal, then a director. He came to work for the school system, he says, because "I wanted to get into teaching," and in five years he hopes to be superintendent of schools. Cavaliere described his job in substantive terms. He said that he had responsibility "for the total educational program of the school system" and went on to describe a series of specific things that that entailed. He continued:

> I use most of my time, at least in thinking, in terms of assessing what's going on. Try to get a handle on the schools. What I see myself doing next, in the summer and even into next September, is sitting down with the administration in each building and saying "Look, we need to establish some definite curriculum objectives for your building, things to work on." Work out a mutually agreeable set of objectives and some approaches and some indicators and start working that way. Generally going toward the kind of program the Board of Education has committed itself to, an individualized program where we try to provide as many different options for kids to learn things. We try to accommodate as many learning styles as possible and skill development using a continuous progress model, which is kids move at the pace that is appropriate for them.

His goals for his job are very specific: to establish a system to evaluate educational programs, to make the secondary school curriculum more responsive to the needs of stu-

---

13. The names of these individuals as well as some details have been changed to camouflage their identities.

dents, and to develop a more systematic way to handle staff development. Not surprisingly, the rewards Cavaliere gets from his job are also substantive: "The opportunity to do some things I have always wanted to do. When you sit there, when you are in a school, as administrator, as a teacher . . . there are things you see and very often you just can't get done. . . . Every now and then I have to remind myself here that I can do it. Ah, that's been good." On the down side, Cavaliere doesn't like the twelve-hour days and the sixty-hour weeks. He also doesn't like the fact that "there are times when one has to simply listen to people who have a pet peeve—sometimes on the board of education—and bite your tongue." His biggest problem is realizing that he has to limit his objectives, establish priorities, and accept the fact that there are things that he wants to accomplish in the school system that he will never get to.

Ted McCann of the fire department has a much different view of his job—he is a worker. He is a high school graduate who has been with the fire department for twenty-eight years. Before coming to the fire department he was in the army and worked in a lumber mill. He joined the fire department because his father was a fireman. Now a deputy chief, McCann doesn't have "any ambitions to go much higher than I am right now". In five years he hopes to be retired. McCann's description of his job is very different from Cavaliere's: "It's a good job, it pays well, it's hard at times but it's not hard all of the time. Right now, the way we work [is] three days on and three days off, and three nights on and three nights off. It gives me a lot of time to myself at home. I only work three nights out of twelve. . . . I have plenty of time to work around the house. . . . It's a good job. It's been damn good to me. It raised my brother and sister and myself and it's also raised my seven children." McCann's dislikes and problems are equally personal: "Our choice of man-power and so forth is limited. It's a civil service job. And then on top of that now that minorities are involved in it and you have to have somebody [of a particular race or ethnicity]. I tried to get my son on the job, and would you believe I couldn't get him on?" Turning to his problems on the job McCann discussed changes he had seen over the years in the people he works with:

> The fire department business used to be esprit de corps once before. One company competing against another company. This day and age is a little different, you have to do a lot of pushing, shoving to get people to do things. And of course the younger generation today, like we have problems with haircuts, this and that you know, the world has turned. When you first came here discipline was unbelieveable. Today of course the union is much stronger. . . . like I say, the esprit de corps is gone.

Sally Warner provides a contrast to both Cavaliere and McCann. Warner is an administrator at heart. When I spoke to her, she had been at the housing authority for a year and a half. Before that she had worked at the city's redevelopment agency. She came to the housing authority because she thought it would be "an opportunity to really focus in on one thing, being responsible for one thing, implement it and so on". Warner has what she sarcastically describes as a "very useful B.A. in sociology," and in five years she expects to be doing "anything administrative." Warner describes her job as "getting things right." She goes on to describe what that means:

> There's a new policy out—how are we going to implement it? How is it going to affect us? How are we going to transmit it to other people in our organization? How do we make sure that everybody is implementing it uniformly? So we don't really do these things . . . we just figure out what day we ought to start having that happen, and how we ought to call

people in, and what the procedure should be and how many
training sessions there ought to be for managers before that
happens, and should it be written down so there's something
they can refer to if they forget part of it and what should
that be written down in. Should it be in a handbook or
should it be put in an existing policy, or that kind of thing.
And that's really how I see my job.

Warner's sense of herself as an administrator comes out
equally clearly when she discusses the rewards she gets
from her job:

Getting things done, that's the biggest reward. That's something. There will be a situation where we call each of the
project offices and ask the same question, and get five different answers as to how it's being handled, and it's the satisfaction of knowing that four of them are doing it wrong,
and one is only doing it half right. And by getting everyone
together and writing it down and having a meeting and discussing it, finally, four do it right and one still does it wrong.
And just the sense that you do bring some uniformity.

Warner continues with much the same administrative
themes when she describes what she does not like about
her job. "I think since I've been here in the area of management, there have been continual problems. Unfilled
positions that have gone unfilled for many months and
indefinite absences at relatively high supervisory levels
which just create a lot of gaps for people. . . . Getting that
resolved would change a lot of things. It would certainly
provide more consistency."

These three administrators are eloquent examples of
the three core identities, but the way they view their jobs
is not substantially different from that of most of their
agency colleagues. The relationship between core identity
and policy area is seen in the accompanying table. The
fourth category in this table, staff professional, covers six
respondents who fit none of the dominant modes. On

Core Identity and Policy Area

	Education	Fire	Housing
Substantive expert	15	1	2
Worker	1	8	0
Administrator	0	0	6
Staff professional	2	2	2

Note: Core identity was derived by considering responses from the entire interview and then assigning an overall code.

close inspection, these proved to be individuals whose jobs differed significantly from the primary technology of their agency. Two were accountants; two ran the separate marshal's office (essentially a regulatory and arson investigation agency) in the fire department; one ran the security department in the housing authority; and the last was in charge of physical plant for the school system. Each of these people was a fish in someone else's technological water. It is not surprising that their core identities do not match those of their fellow bureaucrats.

CORE IDENTITY AND RESISTANCE TO CONTROL

More is at stake in core identities than the fact that firemen look at their jobs differently than educators do. A bureaucrat's core identity defines the sources of satisfaction a bureaucrat derives from his or her job, and the central contribution the bureaucrat sees him or herself making to it. As a result core identities are the source of the first element of the bureaucrats' perceptual filter: the strenuous resistance of any control effort that threatens the core identity. Just as these identities varied across policy areas among the bureaucrats I spoke with, so too did the bureaucrats' responses to different forms of intervention and their assessments of the costs of control.

Experts derive their primary satisfaction from the substance of their work and from their ability to apply their expertise to solve substantive problems. Control is likely to become problematic for experts when it is imposed by actors who do not understand the specialized technology of the policy area. Since fellow experts are the only people with the requisite knowledge, they are the only actors who can legitimately constrain the substance of bureaucratic decision making.[14] In the eyes of experts, substantive constraint by nonexperts—that is, by virtually all political actors—is likely to bring with it potentially high effectiveness costs to the agency. Not understanding the technology, these nonexperts might well impose the wrong constraint.

Educators are the prime examples of substantive experts among the bureaucrats I spoke with. Their most vehement judgments about outside intervention are reserved for substantive meddling by nonexperts. Unfortunately for would-be controllers, this is a capacious net. A common theme raised by educators was the comparison of educational experts with other professionals, a comparison that was intended to discredit nonprofessional intervention.[15] In speaking about the mayor and

14. Douglas Yates calls this guild professionalism (Yates, *Bureaucratic Democracy* [Cambridge MA: Harvard University Press, 1982], chap. 3).

15. Others have found similar sentiments among educators. Dale Mann, for example, writes that "administrators feel that their greater store of knowledge franchises and legitimates their decisions just as surely as it disenfranchises and makes illegitimate the decisional participation of the lay person. The professional litany reinforces such attitudes by teaching that people who are not professionals are ipso facto not competent to participate in 'professional' education decisions" (Mann, "Democratic Theory and Public Participation in Educational Policy Decision Making," in Frederick M. Wirt, ed., *The Polity of the School* [Lexington MA: Lexington Books, 1975], p. 9). Robert K. Yin and Douglas Yates argue that a high degree of professionalism is a major impediment to opening up a service bureaucracy to control (*Street-Level Governments* [Lexing-

other elected officials, one educator told me, "I don't think they should have a great deal of influence on the department of education because we are, you know, so-called experts in this area. We've spent our life in this area, working in it and studying it." The board of education is similarly excluded from significant substantive influence. In the words of another administrator, "How can you tell your surgeon how to remove your appendix? This is really kind of silly, isn't it? Or why should you go to your attorney on a business venture, for example, for advice, and then turn around and tell the attorney what he should do?" A third expounded on the theme of the importance of professionalism at considerable length.

> I have seen the tendency to consider the department of education as just one other municipal office. And when that occurs, I see a lessening of a professional aura about the school system. . . . Over time one has seen the attempts of politicians, some of them are just cigar store owners you know, . . . as the result of some favors owed them in the ward, gravitating to elected official positions. Then they think by grace of a ballot, they suddenly recruit the wisdom, the knowledge that goes with two or three degrees held by the teachers. I'm not an elitist, and I generally hold to egalitarian concepts, but it seems to me that there's a particular point where one gets a little foolish.

If the board, the mayor, and other elected officials are excluded from substantive control on the grounds that they are not professional, it should not be surprising that parents are excluded as well. As one educator explained, the parent "with a little higher education who becomes involved can sometimes become a real problem to the system. They honestly, really believe that they know more

---

ton MA: Lexington Books, 1975], pp. 9–10). More generally, Peter Blau and W. Richard Scott argue that professional service requires the exclusion of client wishes (*Formal Organizations* [London: Routledge and Kegan Paul, 1963], pp. 51–52).

about it than the professionals do, and this is a professional world."

Educators are surely not the only bureaucrats who resent outside interference in the substance of their work. But they are generally more reluctant than bureaucrats working in less specialized fields to admit the possibility that outsiders might be able to understand their work. A bureaucrat in the housing authority was hesitant about according the board of commissioners a substantive role, but suggested that "someone with the knowledge could be an initiator, as long as they know what they are doing." A fire administrator went much further in talking about his board. "The chief himself knows the runnings of the department. Along with the gentlemen that are the commissioners, their knowledge, along with the chief's knowledge, together make a good decision." And another fire administrator saw potential competence among ordinary citizens. "It's their community. I think they should be involved . . . if they . . . know actually what it takes to operate a municipality, departments and all. Definitely if they are up on it and know just what they believe is right, they have the right to voice their opinion." As we shall shortly see, access doors to the fire and housing departments can slam shut quite firmly, but lack of expertise is usually not the precipitating factor.

The broader the claim of expertise, the harder it is to constrain "expert" bureaucrats. When bureaucrats see their expertise as ranging widely, their perceptual filters lead them to reject an extensive array of substantive interventions on the grounds of lack of competence. This was certainly true of many of the educators I spoke with. They included within their zone of expertise many issues that are not narrowly educational and as a result objected to substantive constraint in seemingly nonspecialized areas such as the budget. As one told me, "I would have to say that probably the most distasteful thing is putting an educational program together throughout the entire system for the betterment of youngsters, and reviewing the cost of these programs, and trying to get them as tight as possible—I'm talking about fiscally—and then . . . for example, year before last $32.2 million is what we needed. Well, they gave us $29.7 million. It was impossible to work with that figure." The substantive expert thus claims special competence not only over how a program will be implemented but also over what will be implemented and at what cost.

By contrast, although procedural interventions are not welcomed in the education department, they do not closely touch the bureaucrats' core identity, and are thus not viewed with the alarm that substantive interventions are. An education administrator gave the following example of an appropriate role for the school board:

> The board passed a policy on special education, continuing education for exceptional children. In that policy it gives this department the privilege of determining when the children may, or may not, need continuing education throughout the summer. That policy, as passed by the board, gives us an option. It also sets up a very tight procedure, whereby we have to ensure appropriate input from the personnel who might be involved. The restriction there is that we have to make sure we have appropriate input, but we have the freedom to select the option for the child.

The horizons of the workers in the fire department are more limited than those of the substantive experts in education. They, too, are interested in defending their department against incursions from outside, but the most spirited defense is raised to protect the daily routines of their jobs. Fire fighting is their preserve, but the preserve is a much narrower one than that of education; their core identity lies in the conditions more than in the substance of their work.[16] One fire administrator described his view of the appropriate role for the community: "You can't change the format of the fire department. If you wanted like this hydrant, or if you wanted a hydrant put near your house, or something like that, that's a different story. But as far as actual running of it, no, I don't think that anyone should have a say in that." A second fire administrator also discussed the role of the public, contrasting those areas where citizens might have a say with daily operations where citizen influence must be excluded: "I don't think they should have any role. Except, again, if there was a fire on their property, and they thought that the firemen didn't respond properly, or were late getting there, or did excessive damage beyond the fire damage. Then they would have a legitimate excuse for saying something about it. But insofar as the public interfering with the everyday operation of the department [is concerned], they shouldn't." Still another fire administrator discussed the role of local elected officials: "I think we should accept constructive criticism from the politicians. Not so much in the operations end of the business. Not so much in terms of how to fight fires, but I think we should accept criticism in terms of the more administrative questions, in terms of financial questions. Don't butt in when it comes to fire fighting, but I think it's okay if they say, 'Hey, don't you think you could cut costs somewhat by doing things this way?'" And a fourth talked of a mayoral role, sharply distinguishing between budgetary

16. Weinberg's description of the Massachusetts Department of Public Works is strikingly similar: "The department is also characterized by having a majority of its personnel who are career civil servants. For many of them, a primary concern is the security of their jobs, and their advancement up the civil service ladder. Unlike many departments, where the tenure of employees is much shorter, the issues that move them to political action are as often those involving personal security as those involving policy" (Martha Wagner Weinberg, *Managing the State* [Cambridge MA: MIT Press, 1977], p. 82).

issues and more mundane, but also more important, personnel matters: "He's the mayor. He's going to get involved because he's spending the money, tax money, which is all right, but to that degree. As far as personnel goes, I don't think he should get involved, if you want a good organization." All of these people report serious reservations about external control, but the reservations are markedly different from those of the educators because they are so much more limited and localized. The screening factor is the prevention of disruption of the workplace, not expertise.

For the third core identity, that of the administrator, flexibility is what must be protected. Filters screen out external interventions that limit the ability of the administrator to put together the disparate pieces necessary to create a smoothly functioning organization. As a housing administrator complained, "If this were a private enterprise . . . I think people would view it as a complicated business institution that needs to be run efficiently. But even though we're more complicated in many respects, certainly bigger than many businesses, we're not given anything like the [same] freedom to operate. . . . Everybody under the sun has got to tell us what to do and when to do it." Like substantive experts, administrators voice concern about the effectiveness costs of control. But the objection is not based on the controllers' lack of expertise but on the imposition of undue constraint depriving administrators of needed flexibility.

Bureaucrats in the housing authority speak with passion about their dislike of confining regulations emanating from the federal Department of Housing and Urban Development. They are not objecting to substantive constraints that tell them what to do, but rather to controls that tell them how to do it on a daily basis. One described HUD officials as "very stubborn. They tend to read regulations very strictly and tend not to listen to a housing authority . . . they don't want to listen to a field officer who is much closer to the problems, and knows what kind of problems regulation is going to cause in the housing authority and for the people who live here." Another explained, "I have a lot of trouble watching people from the regional or Washington office of HUD telling us over the phone or in a letter, or whatever, that this is the way you're supposed to be doing it. That's not designed for our needs." A third concurred: "More often than not what it boils down to is some individual in a field office who substitutes his or her judgment for the local official's, who, in my opinion, unless they're abridging a law or regulation, their judgment ought to be supreme vis-à-vis the judgment of the HUD official, who can't possibly have any intimate knowledge of why the judgment's being made, but they constantly do that."

Similar concerns are voiced about the local board of commissioners: "I don't think in any organization, this one included, public or private, that a board ought to make such precise regulations that there's no discretion to act in light of day-to-day circumstances which, in all probability, were not really anticipated at the time the policy was being promulgated."

Three core identities have thus produced three quite different perceptual filters through which bureaucrats view control efforts. In each case external interventions that threaten key aspects of the bureaucratic world are seen as particularly troublesome, but other controls are not. The nature of those problematic interventions, however, varies. For experts, substantive constraint that violates the professional realm is the villain. For workers, it is the workplace routines that must be protected. For administrators, flexibility must be defended from excessive constraint. In this way the dominant technology of a policy area creates a pattern of bureaucratic attitudes that is likely to make certain kinds of democratic control especially difficult to impose.

LEGITIMATE CONTROL

Bureaucratic armor against democratic control is formidable, but it is not impossible to breach. There are chinks in that armor that allow control bureaucrats consider acceptable to pass through unresisted. The bureaucrats I spoke with accept control that they perceive to be either legitimate or useful. The kinds of control that fall into these categories vary, however, depending on the ways the technology and the environment of the bureaucrat's agency mold the bureaucrat's core identity.

For the bureaucrats I spoke with, legitimate control is control wielded by a political actor in an area where that actor is competent. Even though, as I have argued, these bureaucrats rarely look at the issue of democratic control as a normative question about the proper ordering of political institutions, their work-oriented perspective leads them to categories very similar to some of those developed from the normative perspective. Bureaucrats, too, are concerned with the competence of their controllers and with the way in which that competence affects their agency's effectiveness. We have just seen that control bureaucrats perceive as impinging on their core identity is likely to be disliked strongly. But bureaucrats also perceive islands of competence outside their own walls. Such competence is the key to the bureaucrats' perception of some forms of control as legitimate.

Competence is not commonly ascribed by the bureaucrats to their would-be controllers. Where, as in education, the core identity leads to sweepingly broad claims of autonomy, controllers' competence is seldom acknowledged. Elsewhere the potential for control is brighter. When bureaucrats realize that would-be controllers are vitally affected by bureaucratic behavior, they are more likely to accept the idea that outsiders know things the bureaucrats do not—that is, the impact of bureaucratic action on others—and thus have some competence in the bureaucrats' realm. Just who is vitally affected and what their special competence is, however, are questions that differ across policy areas.

Most bureaucrats are civil servants, but for the workers in the fire department this is a central part of their identity; their civil servant status gives them the security and salary they prize. Because their civil service status is salient to them, these bureaucrats are aware of their financial relationship to the larger city administration. They realize that officials with responsibility for the entire city are themselves affected by fire department affairs (particularly by the size of the agency's budget), and that these officials have particular competence in the financial realm. Thus, fire administrators are willing to accord legitimacy to some substantive control by such officials.

In fact, budgetary control is seen as natural. One fire administrator discussed the role of the board of finance that reviews each agency's budget request and then makes a recommendation to the city council: "Somebody has to do it. Someone has to know how many dollars the city has altogether." This same administrator had previously insisted that elected officials knew little about the operation of a fire department and should thus keep out of the operational end of things. But control of the public budget was a different story. Lest one think that such acceptance was the product of largesse toward the fire department, note that the department had experienced a significant cut in its budget the year I was interviewing, as had most city departments.

Fiscal austerity in some ways seems to reinforce these administrators' sense that political control of budgetary matters is legitimate. One high-level bureaucrat in the fire department explained the organization of the department to me as follows:

> There's an assistant chief for administration. And under to-day's economy and tight budgeting, he has to be careful and prudent with the money he spends. He works with what is almost a performance budget. There's a code in the budget for almost every item and you can't move from one code to the other if you have money left over in one category and you need it in another. You have to go through the board of finance and request a change if you want to do that. . . . I think that's a very good idea. It provides a good rein on what you do with money.

Discussing the overall role of elected officials, this same administrator went on:

> The mayor is almost completely responsible. For example, if we're short fifteen men, we have to apply to the personnel appeals board. Now that's an arm of the board of finance, and the mayor is the chairman of the board of finance. So if we're asking that the personnel board release those fifteen positions, the judgment is really the mayor's judgment. [Probe about whether he is happy with this situation.] Yes. The power would have to be somewhere, and it's really senseless for me to decide to put those people back on re-gardless of the total overall budget, because I don't know what the total overall budget needs for this city are. The mayor and the board of finance do.

Thus, because these administrators are very aware that the mayor "picks up the tab," as one told me, they per-ceive that the mayor has some competence appropriate for governance of the department. This perception of competence leads the fire administrators to grant legiti-macy to some forms of mayoral control.

Housing administrators are also aware that their actions constrain those of others, but the source of this awareness differs from that of the workers in the fire department. The mission of public housing is a uniquely public mission, and housing administrators are acutely aware of the consequences of this fact for their jobs. As one explained, "A very large part of what I do, or a very large portion of my work, is generated through federal requirements." Another, comparing his job to one in the private sector, suggested, "Well, certainly they would not be under the constraints that I'm under in that there are certain rules and regulations that we're forced to comply with because of HUD regulations. . . . Also, I would have the ability to be more selective in what I do. . . . I perceive my job if I worked in the private market as being a 9-to-5 job. Now, of course, I work 7 days a week, 365 days a year." Furthermore, a public housing project makes significant demands on local government for services; it also drains local revenues by removing property from the tax rolls. Housing administrators are aware of these considerations if for no other reason than that local officials make them so.

It is not merely the clamor of local and federal officials, however, that causes housing administrators to accede to external control. These administrators accept the public impact of their actions and the fact that others have the competence to assess this impact. They therefore perceive substantive control by officials in those areas of public impact to be legitimate. One housing administrator, for example, explained:

> Often the housing authority gets some of the worst sites, which is not good. But if you look at it from the city's point of view, if it's a good site, and there's going to be some taxable development built there, then they have to look at that. The housing authority would of course want the best sites for its projects and I think that has to be tempered with a view of

what the city also needs. . . . So I think that elected officials should have a say over whether we can indeed build at all. And where we build, because they have to provide schools for the kids, they have to provide all sorts of public services, and I think that that should be considered.

Another administrator made a similar argument.

We are a public agency; we're part of the city. . . . The mayor, whether he wants it or not, generally gets his share of our credits and our debits. . . . I think he ought to help effectuate plans, goals, maybe even programmatic strategies, but on a broad basis. He's not needed to run the place, otherwise we're not needed to be here. But questions like should we be building more housing; if so what type of housing; where; what program if there's a choice of programs available; when? Those are things which I think the mayor is properly responsible for.

Still a third voiced the same opinion.

The city really is, in a lot of ways, its housing stock. . . . Do you go on constructing low-rent housing for as long as there is money available, until 90 percent of your housing stock is low-rent? Do you meet every low-rent housing demand, or do you draw limits to balance low-rent housing with private housing? . . . I think there really should be some account-ability by us to the mayor and to the city council in terms of what we build, in terms of where we build it.

Housing administrators also accord legitimacy to some substantive constraint by their clients, the tenants. The environment of the housing authority is one of a well-defined and limited client group. Unlike fire officials, who serve the entire city, and educators, whose charges are the city's children, housing administrators focus their services on a limited number of low-income tenants. Working with a well-defined client group makes it easier for adminis-trators to identify with their clients and to perceive areas of client competence. These areas may be limited, but they do represent possibilities for legitimate control.

When housing administrators talk about their jobs, their identification with their clients is clear. Over half of them mentioned clients in discussing their goals for their jobs, compared to a third in education and none in fire. One explained, "Certainly I see myself serving, first of all, the immediate people affected, and that's the tenants." Another told me, "I enjoy working here. It's a feeling of being needed because, as you know, about 90 percent of the tenants here are black and are on state welfare." A third asserted, "We're here to serve the public interest, but there of course are different concepts of what the public interest is. My definition of the public interest is probably more geared to low-income people."

Among the housing officials I spoke with being "geared to low-income people" also means granting them a measure of control. Over half of the housing administrators said that clients had some influence over agency policy (only one in education replied similarly, and none in fire). I was told that tenants "should be consulted on anything significant that is going to take place in their project" and that tenants had to have input because "we're controlling their lives, more or less because we're controlling where they live. . . . Since this is ultimately to affect them, I think they should have a big say in what we do and how we do it." A big say does not mean an unlimited say; tenants may have competence, but that competence is bounded in the eyes of the housing administrators. As one quite sympathetic administrator explained, "I don't think they would care what happened to the organization, which, of course, has to be there, has to maintain and manage the units; has to develop new units." Thus some substantive constraint by clients is perceived as legitimate, but only some.

A bureaucratic environment with a well-defined client

group may encourage bureaucrats to see the legitimacy of some client control, but it works to deny legitimacy to control by the community at large. Close client relations lead bureaucrats to perceive clients as competent, but lack of relations with the broader public inhibits bureaucrats from seeing competence elsewhere. The majority of the administrators I spoke with thought the average citizen did not understand what they did, but this view was particularly strong in the housing authority. Every one of the housing administrators saw little citizen understanding (about a third of the administrators in the fire department and almost half of those in education reported at least limited citizen understanding). As one housing administrator put it, "Basically the public, 99.9 percent of them, are unaware and uninvolved." And when the public becomes involved, housing administrators see the public betraying their ignorance by opposing the construction of low-income housing or by complaining about the agency. Two-thirds of the housing administrators reported that they thought the public mostly found fault with their work, compared to slightly more than a third of the educators, and none of the fire administrators.

Housing administrators see little legitimacy in broad public involvement because the competence is not there. One administrator summarized this view by saying that the public's role should be "not much, just because it is such a complicated organization that I think you have to know something about it in order to deal with it. And if you're not either a tenant, who is affected by it, or somebody who knows about the housing authority, I really think it would be inappropriate to have a role." His opinion was seconded by a colleague who asserted: "Other than groups that are like the tenant representative council, I think it would be difficult to be heard. I think it should be difficult because most of them don't under-

stand it, and not understanding it perhaps they don't realize that we have already taken care of their particular
complaint, or were regulated to do just the opposite of
what they are complaining about." Competence-based legitimacy may thus lie with the tenants and at times with
elected officials, but not with the citizenry as a whole.

USEFUL CONTROL: MONEY, INFORMATION, AND COOPERATION

A second group of controls the bureaucrats I spoke with
perceived as acceptable are useful controls. Bureaucrats
are people at work, but people who often do not possess
everything they need to do their jobs well. They may, for
example, not have adequate financial resources to fulfill
their mission; they may be working with a technology that
requires cooperation from clients for success. One way
bureaucrats can obtain what they need to do their jobs is
to give others a measure of control over bureaucratic behavior.[17] Useful control thus joins legitimate control as a
chink in the bureaucratic armor.[18]

17. Writing about organizations in general, Thompson argues that "constraint on the dominant coalition's ability to manipulate premises about outcome preferences occurs when needed inputs are hard to get. Whether the
necessary inputs be client referrals, materials, legitimation, or other, those on
whom the organization is dependent may hold veto power over some possible
goals for the organization. . . . Where such power exists, the organization may
indeed be forced to compromise on or delimit its outcome preferences" (James
D. Thompson, *Organizations in Action* [New York: McGraw-Hill, 1967], p. 138).
    18. For bureaucrats to be willing to accept control in exchange for useful
resources, they have to be interested in doing their job well. Exasperated citizens may at times question the validity of that assumption, but my interviews
with these and other bureaucrats, as well as the findings of other scholars,
convince me that it is a fair one. Michael Lipsky argues quite simply that "street-
level bureaucrats manifestly attempt to do a good job in some way. . . . Street-
level bureaucrats share with others the need to think of themselves in a reasonably favorable light" (Lipsky, *Street-Level Bureaucracy* [New York: Russell
Sage Foundation, 1980], p. 81).

One major resource bureaucrats need is money. Agencies must compete for limited funds, and allies can be enormously useful in such competition.[19] A common way of gaining allies is to cede some autonomy in return for support in budgetary battles.[20] The stronger the mandate an organization has, the less bureaucrats are likely to perceive such exchanges of control for support as necessary. But with fiscal austerity even bureaucrats in traditionally popular agencies such as education perceive control as useful if it facilitates the acquisition of resources.

The educators I spoke with clearly thought about their relationship with elected officials in such utilitarian terms. In the eyes of the bureaucrats a primary role of mayors and council members is to provide support for the school system, and in exchange for that support some scrutiny is acceptable. "Not all of them understand what goes on, but they should certainly be supportive and try to see that we get as many resources as needed to do a job, do the right kind of job. That's one of the major roles they should play. . . . I grant you that they should be very, very scrutinizing in terms of how the money is used, but I think they should be supportive in making sure that it is enough." Most of the bureaucrats realized, however, that obtaining such support was not automatic, and that one way to increase support was to accept involvement by the mayor and council members in the budget-setting pro-

19. See Francis E. Rourke, *Bureaucracy, Politics and Public Policy* (Boston: Little, Brown, 1969), pp. 11–15.

20. If the ally is the client, this describes two sides of the "iron triangle," the third being the legislative subcommittee in charge of the agency. See Rourke, *Bureaucracy, Politics and Public Policy*, and Theodore J. Lowi, *The End of Liberalism* (New York: W. W. Norton, 1969). Joel D. Aberbach and Bert A. Rockman also describe a "symbiotic" relationship between administrators and clients in which the administrators provide access and the clients provide political support (Aberbach and Rockman, "Administrators' Beliefs about the Role of the Public: The Case of American Federal Executives," *Western Political Quarterly* 31 [December 1978]: 504).

cess. This constitutes a procedural constraint, albeit a weak one. One educator advocated

> an ongoing, blue ribbon kind of committee . . . consisting of
> x number of councilmen and someone from the mayor's of-
> fice who will meet with the key group of central office staff
> here and a couple of board members on an ongoing ba-
> sis. . . . The budget has to be ultimately passed by the city
> council, and the mayor controls the council. Not necessarily
> this mayor, any mayor. They have to understand that we
> have recommendations . . . they have to know what we're
> projecting. Then, if they see serious problems with it, that's
> fine, but they have to know that our budget when it comes
> in is going to be a realistic budget. . . . I really think that if
> we can keep those lines of communication open, we can off-
> set a whole lot of problems.

Another administrator told me that he supported in-creased contact between the department of education and the mayor's office because "the very reason our bud-get has been reduced is because of a lack of, say, appre-ciation of the interests of the department by city hall." He felt increased contact would yield increased resources. On a smaller scale, one administrator said that he thought more interaction with the mayor's office might yield "a whole new area of resources to work with our kids. . . . It gives the city administration a better opportunity to see what we're doing in the board of education."

Housing administrators are chronically strapped for resources, and they thus also perceive some weak control as acceptable on utilitarian grounds. Although their pri-mary budget comes from the federal government, these administrators look to the city for supplemental funds. "Financially we find ourselves greatly in need of the city. Our resources are limited, and our ability to improve cer-tain situations really needs outside help." Like the edu-cators, they realize that mayoral support is important to get this help. They also realize that contact with the mayor can be useful to this end. One housing administrator explained, "We do get some community development money to do things in the projects, to upgrade them, to fit better playgrounds, even to help in our development activities. We're asking the city to buy sites for us. And if there's a good relationship between the housing authority and the mayor, then we're much more likely to get that sort of service, to get things from the city." The mayor's political muscle can also be helpful in dealing with the federal government, but the use of this muscle requires giving the mayor some control in return. As another administrator told me, "We cannot always expect elected officials to support us in getting new housing legislation through without them having a say in how policy is going to be set up. I think to ask them to sort of carry the water from the well but not partake of drinking it is sort of asinine." Others put it less colorfully, but many administrators share this perception that accepting control can be a useful way of securing resources.

Citizens also have resources, particularly information, that can be of use to bureaucrats. Bureaucrats working in a complex environment—i.e., one in which there is a great deal of variation in client need—are dependent upon clients for information about their needs. Educators, for example, must tailor their programs to children from very different backgrounds and with substantially different abilities. Obtaining information about where needs lie, however, is not always easy. A limited role for the community in educational governance can be helpful by providing an arena for gathering information.[21] In discussing the community's role one educator argued, "They shouldn't delve too deeply into [the] curriculum. I think

21. Yin and Yates similarly argue that "parent-teacher organizations and activities have provided a basis for the exchange of ideas between servers and served as well as for the potential influence of parents in school policy" (*Street-Level Governments*, p. 65).

they should leave a great deal to the pros. But I think sometimes they do help in neighborhood problems, knowing what the problems are in the particular area, the particular area in which they live." Another educator told me that he thought principals who have school-community councils "are doing the better things in the system." He explained that he saw the councils as a "way to involve the community and get their ideas of how things should be done. I don't always agree with them. I mean, in your own family you don't always agree. But, they are a way of getting some understanding, or some idea of what other people think." Here citizen information serves the same function as the mayor's money: it helps the bureaucrats do a good job. Bureaucrats are willing to accept weak forms of constraint to secure this resource.

Bureaucrats also need cooperation to do their jobs well. Some technologies involve doing things *with* people, not merely to them. For bureaucrats using such a technology, active participation can be vital; bureaucrats may be willing to accept limited control in order to obtain it. Education again provides a clear example. Teaching children involves specialized expertise, but the learning process does not take place solely within the school. For truly effective learning most educators feel they need the cooperation of parents. One way to get this cooperation is to involve parents in participatory structures such as school-community councils. An educator told me that he would like to see such councils become "much more active. Not strong to become a pressure group, though. But strong to be supportive of a school program, to be aware of what it is we're trying to do with and for children so that we can do it together, better." He went on to say that he thought the growth of advisory boards and councils was "very good. Because the children are going to benefit once they recognize that the school personnel, the community, the parents, and everybody is singing out of the same hymn book, saying the same thing. I think that's long overdue." Another administrator, also talking about school-community councils, said, "I would also try to develop with them the feeling that parents have a responsibility to send the person to school in the right frame of mind to learn. . . . I think the parents on the councils should be attending kinds of workshops where people can tell them some of the kinds of things we have as problems and what they can do about it."

Although these councils are quite weak forms of control, they are not mere window dressing. During the period in which I was interviewing, school-community councils played a major role in several personnel decisions, including the ouster of an unpopular principal. Such actions surely go beyond what the administrators consider useful, but the councils were in a position to exercise such influence because the school administrators perceived the existence of the councils to be useful overall.

There are technological elements in housing, too, where active cooperation is vital. In these areas housing administrators mirror their colleagues in education in accepting some forms of control. One told me:

I think a resident organization can only help the housing authority. Most residents share a common viewpoint with the housing authority about what are the problems and what kinds of things should be done about the problems. But without a strong resident group, a strong resident organization, or a strong sense of community among the residents, they take the attitude, "Hey, that's your problem." . . . the financial problems of operating the authority, I think, are really secondary to creating the kind of environment that people can be comfortable living in. Without active participation of the resident population, that environment is never going to come.

Another housing administrator talked about a tenant management experiment in similar terms: "That, of

course, increases their clout tremendously. . . . I think it
may be what we're going to have to come to because if the
tenants don't care about the place they live in, are not
concerned about keeping it clean, keeping it crime free,
keeping the kids in tow, the housing authority just can't
do it."

Bureaucrats may need cooperation even in agencies
that do not deliver human services. Fire administrators
are responsible not only for fighting fires but also for
combatting arson. One fire administrator explained to me
that he would like to establish closer relations with the
community in order to get better cooperation: "That
would help our job a lot. It would help us a lot if they
would tell us when they see people going into vacant
buildings." In this case, of course, the kind of control accepted to achieve cooperation is extremely weak because
the area of needed cooperation is highly limited.

A second form of cooperation that bureaucrats may
need is cooperation with other city agencies. Bureaucrats
who work in an environment of interdependence, whose
work both affects and is affected by that of other local
officials, need cooperation from those officials to do their
jobs well. In the search for this cooperation, weak constraints may be acceptable. The environment of housing
administrators is a clear case of interdependence in two
respects. First, to build and run a housing project, they
need the help of the redevelopment agency, the planning
department, the mayor, the council, and so on. If they are
to get such help, the bureaucrats cannot be completely
isolated. A high-level housing administrator in fact complained, "There's a significant lack of communication between this housing authority and the rest of the city,
which is, I think, to no one's advantage and to everyone's
disadvantage. I think more cooperation is a must. We
don't operate in a vacuum, and, for that matter, nor do

they." In describing his idea of a good administrator, another person in the housing authority said, "I think he's got to become politically and socially involved in his community. He's got to be attuned to what's being done in the community outside the sphere of the housing authority because there might be activity going on out there that's going to affect what you do."

The needs of the clients of the housing authority also contribute to the utility of cooperation to housing administrators. One explained, "There is a population which, in all probability, has a greater need than just housing services. . . . You happen to house a welfare recipient who has a very serious alcohol problem, who, through state welfare, may be being referred to Alcoholics Anonymous. But there's no direct tie with us. . . . It's like this group, which becomes one group in terms of housing, can then be dispersed [to have their other needs fulfilled]." To help service the many needs of her clients, this administrator, along with many of her colleagues, advocated closer cooperation with other service providers. For this reason she perceived some procedural constraints, such as coordinating councils, to be useful.

Other bureaucrats may work in more autonomous environments; but even there pockets of interdependence make cooperation useful. The marshal's office in the fire department, for example, is responsible for certifying that all construction in the city meets the specifications of the fire code. This task means that administrators in the marshal's office must work closely with other city inspectors. As one explained:

> It's very important in any city for all departments to work together where their interests are common. Now, for instance, in a building, we are involved under the state fire safety code. This building is involved under the state basic building code. Now that's the building inspector. Your elec-

trical inspector of the city is responsible, your plumbing inspector is responsible, your zoning officer to see whether the building can be built on the property, your redevelopment agency who looks out for the overall design of the city. . . . So, many departments view the proposals for construction in the city. And we have a very good working relationship on a daily basis.

Anyone who has tried to build a house can probably attest to the difficulty of gaining cooperation from all of these bureaucrats, but this bureaucrat at least saw the utility of cooperation to his own work. He thus saw the need for weak coordinating constraints.

Bureaucrats also need a measure of cooperation from the public to do their jobs well; largely this means having people stay out of their way. The desire to keep people out of their way is, of course, a primary source of bureaucratic resistance to control. It also, however, opens up the possibility that control may be useful. Especially when the bureaucrat's environment includes highly articulated interest groups, keeping people out of the way is not an easy task. If people care about bureaucratic decision making and organize to express that caring, dealing with them can be easier than trying to ignore them.[22] One way to deal with articulated interests is to provide an institutionalized channel for their expression. Such a channel may take the form of an advisory board, community council, or other control mechanism. The primary reason for bureaucrats to support such control mechanisms may be to routinize and mute intervention, but, in so doing, they accept at least weak control.[23]

22. "When the core technology of an organization must be employed on dynamic human objects, the outcome is in part determined by those human objects; and if they hold opposing outcome preferences, some compromise is likely," Thompson argues (*Organizations in Action*, p. 137).

23. David B. Truman similarly suggests that agencies may actively seek to create advisory committees as a way to gain compliance with agency decision making (Truman, *The Governmental Process* [New York: Knopf, 1951],

Educators I spoke with saw two such uses for community involvement. The first was to provide order to the demands coming from the community. One administrator explained, "I believe in structured citizen involvement where you have a mechanism by which you ensure that at each school you have elective councils. This to me does away with the adhocracy that comes out of the woodwork every time you have a crisis." Councils also provide a way of getting people "on board" in advance.

> If you can involve people before the fact in as much policy making as you can, the ultimate result will be to your benefit. To give you a classic example, we have a discipline code. . . . This was developed with the full cooperation of the community, teachers, students, and principals. When that thing went into effect the beauty of that code was the kids couldn't get upset. . . . They had kids come in and testify. Parents couldn't get upset, the PTO was involved. The school councils were involved. . . . It made it very, very amenable, that policy, for implementation purposes.

Housing administrators saw similar uses for tenant organizations. One suggested, "You need to learn to adjust to tenant criticism of changes. Tenant organizations can play an important role, an extension of what we are. They can be emissaries and peace makers."

Even the fire department occasionally needs peace, and when it does, control can be useful. Because of their regulatory role, administrators in the marshal's office work in an environment of well-articulated interests. Builders are rarely indifferent to the added construction costs that the fire code imposes. As one administrator explained,

---

pp. 458–59). On the same point, see also Ezra Suleiman, *Politics, Power, and Bureaucracy in France* (Princeton: Princeton University Press, 1974), p. 327. Aberbach, Putnam, and Rockman recently reported that bureaucrats perform the role of "interest brokers in national politics." They explain that bureaucrats "inhabit an environment in which there are close and continuing relationships with organizations directly affected by administrative actions" (*Bureaucrats and Politicians*, p. 90).

"Just about everyone comes in. Lawyers come in to talk about fire cases, and just about everyone as I stop and think about it. We're truly a public department." Not surprisingly, administrators in this office see a use for consultative procedures that their colleagues elsewhere in the fire department do not. One argued, "The more involvement . . . the greater they understand our problem. So, if you have to make a decision, at least they understand why."

I have now identified three components of the perceptual filters through which bureaucrats view their world. The first is derived from the bureaucrat's core identity and serves to block interventions bureaucrats see as particularly threatening. This component thus reinforces the tendencies to resistance discussed in chapter 4. The other two components of the filter, however, provide hope to those interested in democratically controlling bureaucracy. One component of the filter causes bureaucrats to perceive some control as legitimate; the other component causes them to perceive certain controls as useful.

Capitalizing on bureaucratic perceptions of legitimacy and utility, however, places demands on the would-be controller. The mantle of legitimacy is a thin one, given bureaucrats' overall insensitivity to their political role. Bureaucrats bestow the mantle because they perceive controllers to be competent. If, however, controllers repeatedly act in ways that belie this perception, the mantle is likely to be withdrawn. Bureaucratic perceptions of utility are contingent on desired resources in fact being provided. If, for example, bureaucrats are to accept citizen participation, they must receive the money, information, or cooperation they expect in return. Consideration of perceptual filters therefore provides a guide not only to when political actors are likely to win skirmishes with bureaucrats but also to how they might successfully fight them.

Once again, however, we see that bureaucrats do not look at the issue of democratic control in the same way that potential controllers might. For each set of actors differences among policy areas play an important role, but it is not the same role. As I argued in chapter 5, differences in the technologies and environments of policy areas affect the assumptions on which control is based and the likelihood that the costs of control will arise. These differences should be an important element in any choice of control mechanism. Bureaucrats, on the other hand, rarely think of democratic control as an issue about how a democratic government should be structured, but rather as something that hinders or helps them as they do their jobs. Differences in the technologies and environments in which they work affect what bureaucrats see as hindering and what they see as helpful.

At times these different perspectives lead bureaucrats and controllers to ask similar questions; most notably, How competent are outsiders at governing in a policy area? At such times similar considerations of technological specialization and certainty and of environmental complexity, stability, and interdependence come into play. The bureaucrats I spoke with virtually never used those terms, but that in essence was what they were saying when they spoke of their substantive expertise or their need for flexibility.

Asking the same question does not, of course, mean arriving at the same answer. There are surely instances when an observer would disagree with bureaucrats' evaluation of the competence of others. Some such disagreements may be a result of the bureaucrats' perceptions being clouded by their own self-interest; others may be a product of their experience. In the latter case the observer might want to alter his or her assumptions, but in either case the terms of debate are similar.

At other times the two perspectives diverge sharply. Since bureaucrats do not approach the issue of democratic control as a question of democratic structure, it should not be surprising that they do not consider the issue in terms of the role of democratic government. It would have been equally surprising to have heard the bureaucrats express varying concerns about the ability of controllers to enforce constraint, which is hardly something desirable from the perspective of the bureaucrats.

Each of these perspectives is vital to a full understanding of the problem of controlling bureaucracies and to a choice among control mechanisms. Controllers must consider both what they want and what it is possible to achieve, and they must consider each in a specific policy context. That is the task of choosing and improving control.

7

CHOOSING CONTROL
AND IMPROVING CONTROL

Close inspection has revealed that democratic control of bureaucracy is neither analytically simple nor easy to achieve. Yet the goal is critically important for achieving a truly democratic government. In this chapter I focus on three related lessons from this research: the need to think about control in a differentiated fashion, the need to understand the broader context in which control is exercised, and the need to adopt a strategic perspective on the task of controlling bureaucracies.

THE MANY FACES OF CONTROL

Everybody complains about uncontrolled bureaucracies, and many think that they can do something about them. What that something is, however, varies considerably. One of my major tasks in this book has been to illuminate this variation. Democratic control of bureaucracy has many faces. It is a school board instructing the superintendent to emphasize basic skills in the elementary grades; it is a mayor instructing a fire chief to decide which station to close only after holding public hearings; it is a law requiring that housing authorities work with tenant councils to develop new maintenance policies; it is Congress instructing the secretary of agriculture as to who shall be eligible for food stamps; it is the president requesting the National Endowment for the Arts to avoid concentrating its grants in big cities. There are many different ways to reconcile bureaucracy with democracy. Attention to only one will blind would-be controllers to the complexity of democratic control. Controllers must decide how they will exercise control, what values they will pursue, and what costs they will tolerate. They must also make these choices in the context of particular policy arenas that differ from one another in important ways.

First, controllers must choose among multiple means of constraining bureaucratic behavior. One set of choices involves the question of whether the limits placed on acceptable behavior involve the procedures bureaucrats use to make decisions or the actual substance of those decisions. In the first case control is exercised over the way bureaucrats decide, as the mayor does by requiring the fire chief to hold hearings. In the second case, as when the school board directs the superintendent to emphasize basic skills, control is exercised over what those decisions are.

A second choice involves the extent to which bureaucrats are constrained. Controls run the gamut from loose, ruling out a very limited set of options, to tight, ruling in an equally limited set. The president is exerting loose control over the National Endowment for the Arts when he tells it to avoid concentrating grants. Congress tightly constrains the Department of Agriculture when it specifies precise eligibility requirements for food stamps.

Controllers must also face a set of choices concerning their own beliefs about democracy. Control over crucial policy-making institutions such as bureaucracies is integral to the proper functioning of a democracy. Since the content of the idea of a properly functioning democracy is itself widely disputed, however, would-be controllers must choose which democratic beliefs they will predicate control upon. They must come to grips with how capable they think citizens are of governing themselves, and, more specifically, with how capable citizens and their elected officials are compared to bureaucrats. They must also position themselves between two contrasting reasons for having a democratic government—one primarily liberty-seeking, the other action-seeking. The first emphasizes the protection of the rights of the individual; the second is primarily concerned with the state as a vehicle for achieving the will of the majority of its citizens.

Controlling bureaucracies is rarely a costless enterprise. Controllers must balance the benefits of control against at least three kinds of costs. First, constraining the range of acceptable bureaucratic behavior will at times impair the ability of an agency to carry out its mission. The bureaucracy will fail to attain its original objectives as well as it otherwise might; constraint creates a cost to bureaucratic effectiveness. Second, controllers may find it difficult to determine whether bureaucrats have made a good faith effort to act within the bounds of a constraint. Under these circumstances, they may be reluctant to impose sanctions because they do not want to penalize the bureaucrats for conditions beyond their control. As a result there will be a cost in the controllers' ability to enforce constraint. Controllers who do enforce the constraint may create resentment (or worse) among bureaucrats who think they are being penalized for things beyond their control. Third, controllers frequently encounter resistance from the bureaucrats themselves. When this happens control will be difficult to bring about and may exact a heavy cost to the controller's resources. In the extreme, the controller may abandon the attempt at constraint in order to husband resources for other uses.

A differentiated understanding of the problem of democratic control is not, however, necessarily an unsystematic one. Although this may seem to be a daunting set of choices, a fundamental logic links different kinds of constraint with different democratic values and different costs.

Democratic beliefs are linked to different kinds of constraint through a coherence of vision. Tight constraint of bureaucratic behavior presumes that citizens or their elected officials are capable of making detailed decisions about the work of a bureaucracy. Weak constraint presumes the opposite. An intermediate zone demarcates the belief that competence is widely shared, and that there is no single best way for government to proceed. The choice to constrain the substance of bureaucratic decisions proceeds from the idea that democratic government exists to serve popular ends. In contrast, the choice to control the procedures bureaucrats use to make decisions emanates from the idea that a democratic government is one that safeguards the liberties of its citizens.

The logic that links constraint with costs is one of probability. Tight constraint of bureaucratic behavior leaves little room for flexibility or for the exercise of bureaucratic expertise. It is thus more likely to incur costs to agency effectiveness. Inasmuch as factors beyond the bureaucrat's control are more likely to prevent the achievement of specified goals than they are to prevent the implementation of specified procedures, enforcement costs are more likely to arise when the substance of bureaucratic decisions is constrained.

The structure of choice among potential control mechanisms is constant, but the policy arenas in which the controller must make those choices vary considerably. Variations both in the technology bureaucrats manipulate and the environment in which they operate mean that the same choices about values and costs may not be appropriate for all bureaucracies.

Differences among policy areas in technology and environment may lead controllers to different assessments of the relative capabilities of citizens, elected officials, and bureaucrats. In areas involving highly specialized expertise, for example, bureaucrats often have a greater advantage vis-à-vis citizens and elected officials than in areas where the technology is simpler and more accessible. Differences in technology and environment may also affect the importance controllers attribute to liberty and popular action as goals for a particular policy arena. For example, controllers may give greater importance to liberty in policy environments characterized by substantial goal conflict and more emphasis on accomplishing substantive goals in policy environments where there is considerable agreement on policy ends.

Technological and environmental variation can also affect the likelihood that control will create enforcement or effectiveness costs. For example, policy areas with highly uncertain technologies are more susceptible to the effectiveness problems associated with tight constraints because the uncertainty of the technology means that bureaucrats need considerable latitude to try various approaches to solving a problem. Where technology is certain, controllers are more likely to know how bureaucrats can achieve agency goals and can therefore specify detailed behavior without impairing the work of the agency.

Controllers are not alone in assessing the likely effects of control. Bureaucrats, too, have a vital interest in efforts to control them and potent resources to resist that control. Their stake lies in their political preferences, professional values, and day-to-day work experience; at times it involves their very careers. The likelihood of bureaucrats resisting particular kinds of control also depends on the policy arena involved. Bureaucrats working with different technologies and in different environments tend to have quite different attitudes about their jobs. These attitudes, in turn, have consequences for the kinds of control bureaucrats resist and the kinds of control they accept. As we saw in chapter 6, for example, educational administrators see themselves as masters of a specialized technology; thus they consider themselves to be uniquely competent to make decisions about a broad range of issues. Their colleagues in fire and housing see their monopoly of expertise extending over a more limited domain. They are more likely to attribute competence to elected officials, and as a result are more willing to accept some external controls.

Bureaucratic resistance is certainly a force that makes control more costly to exercise, but it is not only that. Although some complaints are sheer self-interest, bureaucrats also express views about control that reflect an on-the-scene understanding of the consequences of control, and so call attention to other costs of control. In this way, bureaucratic attitudes illuminate not only what is possible but also what is desirable. Educators *do* possess substantive expertise, and their plaints remind us that tight constraints on the substance of educational decisions may indeed impose effectiveness costs on the work of an agency. Similarly, housing administrators insist on their need for flexibility because of the real technological demands of their work. Tight procedural constraints that deprive them of flexibility may seriously undermine their effectiveness.

Would-be controllers have difficult choices to make. Choosing a control mechanism ideally involves understanding the means available, the values at stake, and the probable costs. It also involves calibrating decisions to specific policy arenas. Controllers who approach this task ignoring such differentiation lose the benefit of the richness a differentiated understanding of control provides. At times they may achieve their goals in any case, but those who pursue a single vision of control often limit their own ability to achieve those goals.

THE CONTEXT OF CONTROL

No form of democratic control of bureaucracy exists in a vacuum; all are embedded in a broader political context. Control is exercised by citizens, legislators, or elected executives who play many roles besides controlling bureaucrats. Since these roles are not independent of one another, controlling bureaucrats cannot be looked at in isolation from other aspects of the political system. This embeddedness in the political context is important in at least two ways. First, control brings with it both costs and benefits that ripple through the political system. Second, the effectiveness of individual control mechanisms is often affected by conditions elsewhere in the political system. Our ability to control bureaucracies is limited by the basic attributes of our political system. Thus, a second lesson of this book for would-be controllers is that they must be sensitive to the context in which control takes place.

Controlling bureaucracies can create considerable opportunity costs for controllers. It requires time and effort both to formulate constraints and then to monitor bureaucrats to see that they are followed. This time and effort could be directed to other endeavors. One of the reasons citizens delegate power to representatives and representatives delegate power to bureaucrats is to avoid having to make all the decisions.[1] The more decisions bureaucrats are free to make on their own, the fewer citizens or their representatives must make. Conversely, the more tightly bureaucratic behavior is constrained, the greater the demands placed on citizens or their representatives. Since affecting governmental decision making is a peripheral concern for most citizens, and since controlling bureaucracies is only one of many activities public officials pursue, the opportunity costs of tight constraint can be significant. A president who spends a great deal of time supervising the details of the day-to-day operation of an agency is a president who has less time to spend ensuring the passage of a legislative program.[2] Citizens who choose to vote on who will be awarded a city's recycling contract instead of having the decision made by bureaucrats are citizens who have less time to consider whom to elect to public office, as well as less time to devote to activities outside politics.

On the other hand, controlling bureaucracies can also bring benefits beyond the exercise of constraint. When citizens sit on review boards that oversee an agency's work, for example, they are controlling a bureaucracy; but they are also participating in governing themselves. To some theorists, the act of participating is more valuable than the control of bureaucracy it brings. They believe that participation itself achieves such desirable ends

---

1. Robert A. Dahl calls this the criterion of economy and discusses it in *After the Revolution?* (New Haven: Yale University Press, 1974).

2. Herbert Kaufman, writing about intraorganizational control, makes an analogous point. He argues the attempt to monitor subordinate behavior closely "obliges executives to divert their attention and energies from strategic problems of policy and of external relations to details of internal operations. In short, it absorbs a higher proportion of organizational resources" (Kaufman, *Administrative Feedback* [Washington DC: Brookings Institution, 1973], p. 54).

as the creation of a healthy and fulfilled citizenry.[3] For them the control-related costs of participatory institutions may fade in importance compared to the broader benefits they create. Similarly, when client groups play a role in agency affairs, they are contributing to the control of bureaucracy and also gaining recognition as significant groups in society. Those who place great value on the latter benefit may choose control strategies more for their consequences for the groups involved than for their impact on bureaucratic power. External control may also serve other functions within the bureaucratic context itself. Citizen participation, for example, may legitimate bureaucratic activities even if these activities are merely explained to the participants and not changed by them.[4]

By the same token, however, other aspects of the political context enter into the success of mechanisms for controlling bureaucracy. When ordinary citizens are asked to participate in overseeing bureaucracies, the same factors that discourage them from political participation in general are likely to discourage them from participation in the control of bureaucracy. When interest groups are integrated into the processes of agency governance, the po-

3. Rousseau was probably the foremost proponent of this view. As Carole Pateman explains: "Rousseau's entire political theory hinges on the individual participation of each citizen in political decision making and in his theory participation is very much more than a protective adjunct to a set of institutional arrangements; it also has a psychological effect on the participants, ensuring that there is a continuing interrelationship between the working of institutions and the psychological qualities and attitudes of individuals interacting with them" (Pateman, *Participation and Democratic Theory* [Cambridge: Cambridge University Press, 1970], p. 22).

4. In *Bureaucratic Justice* (New Haven: Yale University Press, 1983), p. 140, Jerry L. Mashaw suggests that this may be one benefit of participation in disability decision making. Daniel A. Mazmanian and Jeanne Nienaber make a similar point about the Army Corps of Engineers in *Can Organizations Change? Environmental Protection, Citizen Participation and the Corps of Engineers* (Washington DC: Brookings Institution, 1979).

litical forces that encourage only some groups to organize will affect the way democratic control of bureaucracy is achieved. When members of Congress control bureaucrats, fragmentation in Congress and the electoral incentives members face will affect the way they do so.[5]

As we saw in chapter 2, political reality can clash with normative beliefs, and when that clash occurs, control mechanisms may malfunction. Control strategies that involve strong substantive constraint by legislators, for example, normally presume that legislators will act to secure general interests, or, alternatively, will act to resolve goal conflicts that might produce conflicting constraints. If legislators' incentives impel them to pursue particularistic interests, however, close legislative control of bureaucrats cannot achieve the values expected from it. Furthermore, such behavior may reinforce the bureaucrats' perception that politicians pursue only narrow self-interest. This entrenches the bureaucrats' conviction that control by elected officials should be resisted. Jerry Mashaw contends that legislative control, in fact, makes many of the problems with the bureaucracy in the Social Security administration worse, not better. He argues: "If bureaucracy in the pejorative sense of insular, rigid, and insensitive is the problem, then, as we have seen, reform in the image of democratic ideals is not the solution for a program like the DI [disability insurance] program. It is re-

---

5. Douglas T. Yates argues that congressional control of bureaucracy is diluted by the fragmentation of the committee system (Yates, *Bureaucratic Democracy* [Cambridge MA: Harvard University Press, 1982], p. 159). More generally, James Q. Wilson maintains that "the particularistic and localistic nature of American democracy has created a particularistic and client-serving administration. If our bureaucracy often serves special interests and is subject to no central direction, it is because our legislature often serves special interests and is subject to no central leadership" (Wilson, "The Rise of the Bureaucratic State," in Nathan Glazer and Irving Kristol, eds., *The American Commonwealth, 1976* [New York: Basic Books, 1976], p. 103).

sponsiveness to the democratically constituted legislature that has pushed SSA in 'bureaucratic' directions."[6]

Legislatures, of course, are not the only context in which control takes place. Client-oriented control strategies generally presume that all interests will organize. If, however, some groups in society do not have the political resources to organize, those groups will not be represented in the interplay of interests such strategies presume. Judicial review of bureaucratic decisions is equally limited by the scope of judicial authority and the powers of the courts to enforce their decisions. Moreover, any form of control will be afflicted by contradictory impulses if the political system itself is in conflict over what an agency should do.

In each of these cases, malfunctions in mechanisms designed to control bureaucrats are not the result of narrow flaws in design, but are manifestations of broader political phenomena. At times even an advocate of democratic control might applaud bureaucratic resistance to constraints that seem to serve the private interests of the controller. Such applause is generally rooted in ambivalence about how our political system is working. Championing appointed officials over elected ones is hardly the democratic norm. A dislike for the ways legislators, executives, or citizens seek to control bureaucracies suggests deeper problems with the way those actors wield political power, problems that have ramifications well beyond the issue of controlling bureaucracies. Democratic control of bureaucracy is hardly immune to the forces shaping other aspects of our political system. Often the road to improving control is blocked by the thorny democratic context in which control takes place.

6. Mashaw, *Bureaucratic Justice*, p. 223.

A STRATEGIC APPROACH TO CONTROL

A control relationship is in essence one of inequality. For control to be effective, no matter how it is exercised, the controller must have sufficient resources to induce the object of control to behave in the way the controller wishes. Control becomes difficult when the inequality runs in the opposite direction: when the object of control has greater resources than the would-be controller. In the case of democratic control of bureaucracies, the dominant resource used to exercise control is the controller's formal authority. Elected officials have the legal power to set up mechanisms that constrain the behavior of appointed ones, and they have a monopoly over that power. However, bureaucrats have other resources in considerably greater measure than their would-be controllers. These inequalities serve to hinder, not facilitate control.[7]

Three critical resources possessed in abundance by bureaucrats put them in a favorable position compared to their controllers. First, they have responsibility for making the day-to-day decisions in their agency. Second, because they are on the scene, bureaucrats, more than anyone else, have information about the affairs of their agency. Third, bureaucrats command the resource of substantive expertise: they bring to their work specialized knowledge about how to achieve the ends of the agency.

None of these inequalities is either accidental or perverse; they flow from the very nature of bureaucracy. We

7. In a more general discussion of the problem of control, Robert A. Dahl argues that one of the reasons representatives may not be able to control subsystems is the access of subsystems to resources that impede the exercise of control (Dahl, *Dilemmas of Pluralist Democracy* [New Haven: Yale University Press, 1982], pp. 50–51). Janet A. Weiss and Judith E. Gruber also discuss the point in "Using Knowledge for Control in Fragmented Policy Arenas," *Journal of Policy Analysis and Management* 3 (1984):225–47.

hire bureaucrats because we cannot deliver services alone. Bureaucrats are hired precisely because they are specialists, and they are deliberately given control over agency affairs. We need both their substantive expertise and their undivided attention to conduct the business of government. Alas, these very virtues become liabilities when it comes to exercising democratic control. They create the conditions that give rise to the costs of control.

Bureaucrats are able deliberately to ignore a constraint or to let it slip in the course of the exigencies of agency life because they have the resource of responsibility for day-to-day decision making. When they ignore democratic control they produce the cost of bureaucratic resistance. When they let it slide, they create circumstances that give rise to the problem of enforcing constraint. Having day-to-day responsibility also means that bureaucrats are uniquely qualified to calibrate their actions to changing conditions; tight constraint denies bureaucrats the ability to be as effective as possible. Bureaucratic dominance of all three resources means that bureaucrats are in a privileged position to know what is going on in their agency and how to achieve agency ends. When controllers have limited access to these resources, they are unable to determine accurately what kinds of constraints on bureaucratic behavior will produce the ends they desire. It is this situation that produces the effectiveness cost created by the imposition of the wrong constraint.

Democratic norms ignore the difficulties with such problems of control because they stress the sovereignty of the citizen and the subservience of the bureaucrat. But authority to command bureaucrats guarantees neither that the command will be obeyed nor that control will achieve what the controllers want it to. Because of the abundance of other resources bureaucrats possess, for-

mal authority is not enough to secure control of bureaucracies.[8] A third lesson of this research is thus that controllers must look at control as a strategic problem of
creating and marshaling resources to facilitate the exercise of control.

One strategy for improving the prospects for control is
to use formal authority to force bureaucrats to share their
resources, especially information, with would-be controllers. Michael Lipsky argues for the need "to provide a
better balance of power between street-level workers and
clients". He suggests that one way to do this is to "demys-
tify" bureaucratic processes by providing clients with information such as guides to client rights, maps of the bureaucratic system, and written summaries of agency
actions.[9] Control mechanisms themselves may be designed and used to narrow the resource gap between controllers and bureaucrats by opening up an agency to public examination. "Sunshine" laws that require exposing
some bureaucratic processes to public view, for example,
may be used not merely as a procedural constraint but
also as a way of increasing the amount of information
controllers have about agency affairs. Such increased information may in turn allow for tighter substantive constraints without incurring effectiveness costs, since well-
informed controllers are less likely to impose the wrong
constraints. Similarly, legislatively mandated reporting requirements may serve not merely as a way of overseeing
what bureaucrats have done but also as a way of providing
information about bureaucratic activities to citizens and

---

8. This perspective on authority is similar to that proposed by Chester I.
Barnard. He argues in effect that authority lies in the eye of the beholder and
not in the person of the possessor. As a result he maintains that people cannot
merely be ordered to cooperate but must be induced to (Barnard, *The Functions
of the Executive* [Cambridge MA: Harvard University Press, 1983], chap. 12).

9. Michael Lipsky, *Street-Level Bureaucracy* (New York: Russell Sage Foundation, 1980), p. 195.

interest groups. Armed with the bureaucrats' own information, they may exercise control more effectively.

Would-be controllers can also improve their prospects for control by extending their sights to resources other than formal authority as resources for control. As we saw in chapter 4, the value of democratic control pales in bureaucratic eyes in the light of the demands of their jobs. Thus, a claim by controllers to democratic authority is not a potent resource if bureaucrats see control as threatening other values. But, as we saw in chapter 6, these other values, and particularly the bureaucrat's desire to do a good job, provide a vehicle for the introduction of control. Successful controls are often those that can ride piggyback on the bureaucrats' conception of their self-interest. As William Niskanen argues, "Any public administration reforms that will be both beneficial and enduring must create conditions such that the activities (legal or otherwise) of bureaucrats and review officers, acting in their personal interests, are more nearly consistent with the public interest."[10] One way of making the private interests of bureaucrats converge with the public's interest in control is more explicitly to parlay the resources controllers command and bureaucrats seek into bureaucratic acceptance of control.

Controllers do possess an array of resources potentially useful to bureaucrats. Funding, access to political leaders, information, and cooperation are all things bureaucrats value. All are resources that can ease the process of control. Political executives with close connections to the White House, state house, or city hall may shore up their

10. William A. Niskanen, Jr., *Bureaucracy and Representative Government* (Chicago: Aldine-Atherton, 1971), p. 194. Peter M. Blau similarly argues that public control of bureaucracy hinges upon "converting external dysfunctions into internal needs of the organization that disturb its personnel" (Blau, *The Dynamics of Bureaucracy* [Chicago: University of Chicago Press, 1963], p. 264).

influence within their agency by using those connections to deliver funding, jurisdiction, or other "goods" bureaucrats want.[11] Legislators may gain control of some bureaucratic decisions by being loyal supporters of an agency's budget.[12] Mayors and governors can use discretionary funds to induce bureaucrats to pursue programs they otherwise might not.

Citizens have the resource of cooperation and the threat of disrupting bureaucratic activities if they withhold cooperation.[13] Most bureaucrats would prefer not to have their agency be the object of boycotts and demonstrations, and they may accede to some of the wishes of citizens in order to avoid such pressures. On the positive side, public cooperation can be helpful to bureaucrats. Parents know about their children's needs and have some influence over their children's behavior in school. Tenants can cooperate in maintaining a housing project. Citizens can report suspicious activities to fire officials. All of these resources are valued by bureaucrats, and may thus be converted into a measure of control. Moreover, the strategy of breaking the bureaucratic monopoly on information may augment the effectiveness of these resources. Information about bureaucratic activities may mobilize previously apathetic citizens by informing them of the consequences of bureaucratic action, thereby encouraging them to harness their resources to the task of control.[14]

11. "In every department in every recent administration, one of the chief ways political executives gained support in the bureaucracy was by being, or at least appearing to be, their agency's vigorous spokesman," writes Hugh Heclo (*A Government of Strangers* [Washington DC: Brookings Institution, 1977], p. 196).

12. Douglas Arnold, *Congress and the Bureaucracy* (New Haven: Yale University Press, 1979).

13. Lipsky argues that clients have resources to "impose a variety of low-level costs" on bureaucrats (*Street-Level Bureaucracy*, p. 57).

14. David L. Kirp, for example, notes that a mid-1960s audit of Oakland's Title I expenditures provoked anger, and then mobilization in the black com-

A further strategy for improving the prospects for control is for would-be controllers to create arenas in which their resources can be utilized. If resources are to be transformed into control, bureaucrats must know that would-be controllers have these resources and controllers must have the opportunity to use them.[15] Given the normal proclivity of bureaucrats to keep to themselves, such opportunities are not always easy to find. To promote these opportunities, control structures can be designed to force greater interaction between bureaucrats and citizens or elected officials and in that way facilitate the conversion of resources into the acceptance of control.

Control mechanisms such as advisory boards or consultative committees that provide for such interaction achieve control of bureaucracy in two ways. First, control emerges from the explicit work of the board or committee itself. Second, by creating arenas for interaction, such control mechanisms provide opportunities for informal influence that may go beyond the formal arrangements. For example, school councils are important not only because of their official powers but also because they provide a forum for bringing parents and school administrators together. Such interaction provides parents with an opportunity to proffer their resources of information and cooperation and to express views on how they would like the schools to be run. Because the resources are useful to administrators, they may be willing to listen.

---

munity when it showed that funds had not been targeted at disadvantaged children (Kirp, "Race, Schooling and Interest Politics: The Oakland Story," *School Review* 87, no. 4 [August 1979]: 355–97). More generally Mashaw argues that "a sense of illegitimacy, even outrage, may also have its value in promoting bureaucratic justice" (*Bureaucratic Justice*, p. 142).

15. In *The Logic of Bureaucratic Conduct* (Cambridge: Cambridge University Press, 1982), Albert Breton and Ronald Wintrobe argue for the role of interaction as a vehicle for creating the trust that they assert is essential for exchange to take place.

Listening may in turn result in changed behavior. Having listened, administrators may have new sensitivity to certain problems, enhanced appreciation of parent competence, or simply the desire to keep the parents coming back. Furthermore, to the extent that bureaucrats are controlled by a process of anticipating what citizens will accept and trying to stay within those bounds, listening should improve control by clarifying just where those bounds really are.[16] Mashaw argues that client participation in disability determinations "may help to ensure that the adjudicator 'really listens' to what the claimant thinks is important and that disadvantageous evidence is not accepted without close scrutiny."[17] Institutions such as ombudsmen may also provide an arena for interaction to take place. Thus they can control bureaucrats not merely through their official power to redress grievances but also by providing bureaucrats with valued information about citizen unhappiness.

Arenas for the exchange of resources may also be created through modest administrative restructuring to reduce the insularity of bureaucratic life.[18] As the data in chapter 4 indicate, bureaucrats rarely seek out contact with other public officials or with citizens; the contact they have generally comes from structured interactions such as board meetings, the need to deal with other officials to

16. Anthony Downs argues that pressure on bureaucrats to improve their performance "tends to make each official shift his definition of 'satisfactory performance' closer to the definition held by these external agents. This is the main way in which social agents get a bureau to perform its functions to their satisfaction" (Downs, *Inside Bureaucracy* [Boston: Little, Brown, 1967], p. 193).

17. Mashaw, *Bureaucratic Justice*, p. 140.

18. William R. Dill argues that different organizational environments produce varying levels of informal interaction among organizational members, and that such interaction in turn reduces autonomy (Dill, "Environment as an Influence on Managerial Autonomy", *Administrative Science Quarterly* 2 [March 1958]: 409–43). Mashaw also argues that bureaucracies can be structured "to establish appropriate relationships" among political actors (Mashaw, *Bureaucratic Justice*, p. 158).

secure supplementary funds, or citizen-initiated requests. Since bureaucrats have little time or inclination to consult with others over broad policy issues, they may resist control mechanisms directed to this end. If, however, more contact can be built into daily coping processes, controllers gain an opportunity both to demonstrate their competence to bureaucrats and to offer useful resources. In this way they may gain greater control over bureaucratic behavior. Lipsky, for example, points out that street-level bureaucrats are at times compelled to make their decisions in public "so that they can be exposed to, if not influenced by, the presence of those affected by the decisions. Such policy incorporates the theory that clients are likely to become more a part of the bureaucrats' reference groups if they are present at times when decisions are made."[19] Mashaw makes a similar proposal for structuring "the state agency process so that claimants are as real to adjudicators as are the medical consultants, unit supervisors, bureau chiefs, QA [quality assurance] staff, medical listings, DOT [*Dictionary of Occupational Titles*], DISM [Disability Insurance State Manual], and disability determination forms that make up their daily work environment. The examiners could be forced to talk to claimants, to treat them as important sources of information, to explain their eligibility decisions."[20]

Cross-national research offers strong evidence of the impact of institutional arrangements on bureaucratic autonomy. In a study of seven western democracies, Aberbach, Putnam, and Rockman examine the attitudes of bureaucrats and politicians and the relationships between the two groups. Although they find considerable similarity in the attitudes held by each group across countries,

19. Lipsky, *Street-Level Bureaucracy*, p. 128.
20. Mashaw, *Bureaucratic Justice*, p. 198.

they find noticeable differences in the nature of the linkages in countries with decentralized political systems compared to those with more centralized governments. They conclude: "Bureaucrats *must* do some things and *may* do other things. Attitudes affect what individuals choose to do among the repertoire of those things they *may* do, but what *must* be done is greatly influenced by institutional arrangements. Institutional arrangements that fragment power create conditions of mutual dependence, and mutual dependence in turn encourages interaction between politicians and bureaucrats, because each holds resources valued by the other."[21] Fragmentation does not always hold the answer to bureaucratic insularity. Given enough dispersion of power, bureaucrats can shop for the resources they need without relinquishing control. Under those circumstances concentrating resources in the hands of mayors, councils, or governors may provide the structural lever to force bureaucrats to depend more on elected officials.

CONTROL AS EXCHANGE

By emphasizing the creation of resources and the development of arenas for their strategic use, I have moved away from traditional conceptions of control as based in an authority relationship toward an understanding of control based more on a model of exchange.[22] In an ex-

21. Joel D. Aberbach, Robert D. Putnam, and Bert A. Rockman, *Bureaucrats and Politicians in Western Democracies* (Cambridge MA: Harvard University Press, 1981), p. 236.
22. Charles E. Lindblom discusses three dominant modes of control: exchange, authority, and persuasion. While exchange is generally associated with economic arrangements, we may borrow from Lindblom and consider how this mode of control might be incorporated into strategies for democratic control of bureaucracy (Lindblom, *Politics and Markets* [New York: Basic Books, 1977]).

change model, control results not from political actors telling bureaucrats what to do but from constructing conditions in which bureaucratic behavior is constrained in exchange for resources that bureaucrats seek.[23] Such control emanates from a process of interaction, not from one of orders from above.

Control by exchange, of course, operates against a backdrop of authority. Formal governmental powers provide many of the resources, such as public funds and legal jurisdiction, that are used in exchange. Authority may also provide the threat of worse consequences if exchange is not pursued. Public officials have the authority to strip recalcitrant administrators of their funding and, in some cases, of their jobs. Citizens have the authority to bring a lawsuit against an agency that is uncooperative. Administrators understand this and may often be willing to engage in exchange to avoid such consequences.[24] The two modes of control thus work closely together.

Sensitivity to the prospects for exchange should im-

---

23. Students of both private and public organization have examined exchange as a means for both intraorganizational and interorganizational control. David Jacobs, for example, argues that organizations are dependent on those actors who control items essential to the organization that cannot easily be obtained from other sources. He suggests that organizations will mold their behavior to meet the expectations of those who control such resources (Jacobs, "Dependency and Vulnerability: An Exchange Approach to the Control of Organizations," *Administrative Science Quarterly* 19 [March 1974]: 45–59). Jeffrey Pfeffer and Gerald R. Salancik provide an extended discussion of the role of resource dependence in the control of organizations in *The External Control of Organizations* (New York: Harper and Row, 1978). Albert Breton and Ronald Wintrobe base their entire analysis of bureaucratic conduct on the assumption that bureaucratic relationships are exchange relationships (*The Logic of Bureaucratic Conduct* [Cambridge: Cambridge University Press, 1982].

24. Aberbach, Putnam, and Rockman argue that "constitutionally politicians are everywhere empowered to reject the counsel of bureaucrats, although such rejection is infrequent in practice. Policy making is thus a kind of dialectic, in which the 'law of anticipated reactions' normally governs the behavior of bureaucrats" (*Bureaucrats and Politicians*, p. 248). Peter H. Schuck discusses the use of tort law to control bureaucrats in *Suing Government* (New Haven: Yale University Press, 1983).

prove the design of formal control structures. Thinking in terms of exchange suggests new ways of conceptualizing strategies for democratic control. Orders are augmented or replaced by resources, commands by negotiation. Many of the same control mechanisms may be used, but used in a way that provides resources for exchange or facilitates participation in an exchange process.

The potency of exchange in a bureaucratic context can be seen in a variety of situations. Students of the federal government often decry the insularity of the "iron triangles" linking agencies, congressional subcommittees, and interest groups.[25] Looked at from the perspective developed here, these iron triangles are testimony to the power of exchange through which interest groups and members of Congress are able to affect bureaucratic behavior by providing the agency with needed support. Similarly, in the area of coordination of human service delivery, Janet Weiss has argued for the importance of providing bureaucrats with incentives to change their behavior.[26]

Acceptance and use of exchange are not limited to actors outside the bureaucracy. Bureaucrats themselves often use exchange to supplement their formal authority. "Street-level" bureaucrats need to gain client compliance, and Lipsky argues that they do so "either through the control of resources that the client desires (utilitarian compliance) or . . . through force or the threat of force."[27] Good policemen mix persuasion and help with coercion in the course of their work.[28] Many teachers overcome the

25. See, for example, Francis E. Rourke, *Bureaucracy, Politics and Public Policy* (Boston: Little, Brown, 1969).
26. Janet A. Weiss, "Substance vs. Symbol in Administrative Reform: The Case of Human Services Coordination," *Policy Analysis* 7 (Winter 1981): 21–45.
27. Lipsky, *Street-Level Bureaucracy*, p. 42.
28. See William K. Muir, *Police: Streetcorner Politicians* (Chicago: University of Chicago Press, 1977).

inadequacy of their authority by exchanging the relaxation of some classroom rules for order and concentration by students.[29] In the regulatory arena Eugene Bardach and Robert Kagan observe that "an enforcement official's ability to win cooperation is rooted in the relationship of reciprocity or exchange that he manages to establish."[30] Regulatory inspectors trade responsiveness, forebearance, and information for responsible social behavior on the part of the regulated.[31]

Designing control mechanisms to coincide with bureaucrats' perceptions of their own interests may appear to violate the very premise upon which the need for control is based—i.e., that public actions should be controlled by the citizenry. To an extent this appearance is accurate. Strategic design allows for considerable bureaucratic power in decision making by accepting the facts that bureaucrats have resources for resistance that cannot merely be ordered away and have resources that often make them more able to discern appropriate courses of action than controllers. However, short of a fundamental change in the division of labor in democratic societies that eliminates the very existence of delegated authority, bureaucrats will have these resources and will be in a position to resist controls they do not find acceptable. Ignoring that fact may produce controls that are normatively

29. Mary Haywood Metz, *Classrooms and Corridors* (Berkeley and Los Angeles: University of California Press, 1978), especially pp. 97–116.
30. Eugene Bardach and Robert A. Kagan, *Going by the Book: The Problem of Regulatory Unreasonableness* (Philadelphia: Temple University Press, 1982), p. 130.
31. Bardach and Kagan also contrast what they call indirect regulation with command and control regulation. The latter relies on formal legal authority, whereas many forms of indirect regulation, such as providing citizens with information to be their own inspectors and using liability law, bear a close resemblance to control by exchange (*Going by the Book*, pt. 3).

pleasing but ineffective in practice.[32] Accepting that fact may allow controllers to develop strategies that widen the domain in which bureaucrats are willing to accede to controllers' wishes.[33]

As every chapter in this book has indicated, democratic control of bureaucracy involves complex and difficult choices. These choices are made more difficult by the fact that bureaucrats command resources that controllers need. Fortunately, controllers also have resources that bureaucrats find useful. The road to successful control lies in understanding both the democratic and bureaucratic sides of the problem and carefully crafting efforts so that neither democratic norms nor bureaucratic facts are denied.

32. Heclo argues for the virtues of evoking "conditional cooperation" as opposed to "invoking authority" (*Government of Strangers*, p. 220. Similarly, Martin Landau and Russell Stout, Jr., call for seeking decisions that fall within the "zone of acceptance" of subordinates (Landau and Stout, "To Manage is Not to Control: Or the Folly of Type Two Errors," *Public Administration Review* 39 [1979]:151).

33. Barnard calls this the "zone of indifference" (*Functions of the Executive*, pp. 167–70).

Appendix I:
Sample Interview Schedule

1. How long have you worked for the housing authority?

2. What did you do before that?

3. Why did you come to work for the housing authority?

4. What do you think you'll be doing five years from now?

5. What is your educational background?

6. What was your father's occupation?

7. What was his educational background?

8. Do you belong to a union or professional organization? Is that organization important to you?

9. Would you tell me a little bit about how you see your job? What are its rewards?

   Are there things you dislike about it?
   What are your goals in the job?
   What do you see as the main problems in achieving those goals?

10. Do you think your job is different from similar jobs in the private sector?

11. Are you pretty much free to do what you want to do on the job? Who sets limits?

    What kinds?

12. Whom do you see yourself serving in your job?

> What do they generally want?
>
> How much does it matter to you that they like what you do?

13. Whose opinion about your work do you care most about? On what basis do you think they judge your work?

14. How much influence do you see yourself having over (housing authority) policy?

> Who else do you think has influence?
>
> Are there people or groups who you think have either too much influence or not enough?
>
> How much weight do you think that people like yourself, who are (housing) professionals, should have in decision making, as opposed to people like the mayor and the commissioners?
>
> Would you prefer that policies set by the (housing) commissioners be general ones which allow you a lot of discretion or would you prefer that they be precise?

15. What's your idea of a good (housing) administrator?

> What would be an ideal organizational structure for that administrator to work in?

16. Whom do you talk to about your work?

> Whom do you ask for advice?
>
> Who asks you for advice?

17. How often do you talk to other administrators in the department? Who usually initiates the contact?

> What do you generally talk about?
>
> How often do you talk to people from other city departments? (People from HUD?)
>
> (Housing) commissioners?

People from the mayor's office?
Aldermen?
People from the local political parties?
Representatives of citizens' groups? What groups?
Individual citizens?

18. Do you feel that dealing with individuals and citizens' groups is an important part of your job?

19. Whose opinion makes a difference around this department?

20. Who do you think has a right to a say about what goes on in the department?

    What kinds of decisions do you think community people should be involved in?

21. What do you think people who work for the (housing authority) should be held accountable for? By whom?

22. What kind of role do you think local elected officials should play in the operation of this department?

    Do you think it makes much of a difference who the mayor and council members are in terms of what goes on here?
    What about who the (housing) commissioners are?

23. What kind of role do you think the public should play in the operation of this department?

    Do you think you get much appreciation from the public or do they mostly find fault?
    How much do you think the public cares about what you do? How much do you think the average citizen understands what you do?
    How much public conflict do you think there is over what you do? What is the conflict about?
    How would you like to see the public change to help the department in doing its job?

24. Some people talk about public agencies being un-democratic. Do you think that this is a problem?

    What can be done about it?

25. Another criticism one sometimes hears about public agencies is that they are too responsive to outside pressures and groups. Do you think that this is a problem?

26. A final complaint that people sometimes voice about public agencies is that there's too much "red tape."

    Do you think that that's a problem?
    Do you ever feel hemmed in by rules and regula-tions which keep you from doing a good job?

27. If someone had a suggestion for the department, how would they go about proposing it?

28. What do you see as the major problems facing our cities today? What should government do about them?

    What should ordinary citizens do about them?
    What are the major problems in the area of (hous-ing)?

29. Some people say that different groups in society want different things and are bound to come into conflict with each other. Do you think that this is true?

30. Do you think that there is such a thing as the "public interest"? What is it?

31. What do you see as being the general role of govern-ment?

    What kinds of things do you think government should do?
    What kinds of things do you think government should keep out of?

What do you see as the bigger problem: Too much government action or not enough?

32. What to you are the essentials of a democracy?

33. Are there ways that this city or country could or should be more democratic than it is today?

34. Ideally speaking, what would you say is the proper role for the public in government?

35. In general, do you think that most of the time people know what is best for themselves?

    Who does know best?
    What about in the area of (housing) needs?

36. There's been a good deal of discussion lately about increasing popular participation in, and control over, government. Do you think that this is a good idea?

Appendix II:
Agency Variations in Coded Responses to Selected Questions

	Housing (N = 10)	Fire (N = 11)	Education (N = 18)
How long have you worked for the agency?			
Less than 5 years	60%	0%	0%
5–10 years	30	0	18
11–20 years	0	0	29
Over 20 years	10	100	53
Why did you come to work for the agency?			
Interest in substance of job	50%	45%	88%
Security of job	0	54	0
Experience offered by job	50	0	0
Miscellaneous	0	0	12
What do you see yourself doing five years from now?			
Retired	0%	72%	26%
Same job	20	27	33
Different job, same field	30	0	33

| Same field, private sector | 10 | 0 | 7 |
| Public sector administra-
tion, different field | 40 | 0 | 0 |

Tell me a little bit about how you see your job.

Administrator	60%	18%	83%
Providing technical ser- vice to administrators	0	9	11
Providing substantive service to public	0	9	6
Affective description	40	64	0

What are its rewards? What do you like most?

Working conditions	10%	45%	17%
Providing substantive service	50	45	83
Sense of accomplishment	40	9	0

Are there things you dislike about it?

None	0%	27%	0%
Working conditions	30	55	29
Impediments to delivery of service	30	9	24
Impediments to getting things done	30	0	6
Administrative detail	10	9	41

What would you say your goals are in your job?

| Mention of client | 60% | 0% | 33% |
| No mention of client | 40 | 100 | 67 |

What do you see as the major obstacles to achieving
your goals?

Substantive problems	10%	22%	60%
Organizational factors	80	78	27
Political/community pressure	10	0	13

Do you think your job is very different from similar jobs
in the private sector?

Similar	11%	18%	19%
Different: substance of job	11	27	37
Different: greater freedom in working conditions	22	45	19
Different: statutory restrictions in public sector	44	9	6
Different: political pressures in public sector	11	0	19

Who do you see yourself as serving in your job?

Public	10%	82%	25%
Clients	30	0	44
Mayor	0	9	0
Board	10	0	0
Agency head or staff	40	9	31
Self	10	0	0

Who else has influence (over agency policy)?

Mention of clients	60%	0%	6%
No mention of clients	40	100	94

What is your idea of a good administrator for this agency?*

Manager, decision maker	70%	50%	40%
Substantive expert	20	50	60
Work well with elected officials	20	20	0
Work well with staff, a leader	20	60	47
Work well with clients	40	0	27
Work well with public	10	20	13

How often, on average, do you talk to people from the mayor's office?

Frequently or occasionally	90%	18%	63%
Rarely or never	10	82	37

Do you think you get much appreciation from the public or do they mostly find fault?

Mostly find fault	66%	0%	40%
Mixed appreciation and fault	0	0	20
Mostly appreciation	0	90	40
Other	33	10	0

*Includes multiple responses.

How much do you think the average citizen under-
stands what you do?

Somewhat	11%	22%	23%
Varies	0	11	23
Not much	89	66	54

Index

Aberbach, Joel D., 70n, 150, 187n, 209–10; on bureaucrats and citizens, 97n–98n; on bureaucrats and clients, 179n; on bureaucrats and politicians, 104n, 114n, 209–10, 211n; on democracy, 87n–88n; governance model of, 35n; politics model of, 35n, 45n

Accountability, 11, 18, 19n, 22–23; Birch on, 9n, 11n–12n; in complex environments, 146n; responsibility linked to, 9n, 64n, 65, 66

Action-seeking perspective, 49, 50–54, 193, 195

Administrators, identity as, 153, 157–58, 159, 161–62, 169–71

Advisory boards, 55, 73, 182–83, 186, 198, 207

Affirmative action, 117

Appointees, political, 72–73

Arnold, Douglas, 115n

Attitudes: bureaucrats', 24–26, 85–120, 149–90, 196, 209–10; politicians', 6, 25n, 209–10. See also Norms

Authority, 151n, 203–5, 210, 211, 212–13

Autonomy, bureaucratic, 16, 92–101, 103, 107, 116, 120, 146–47

Bachrach, Peter, 34n, 37

Banfield, Edward C., 75n–76n, 77n, 82n–83n

Bardach, Eugene, 9n, 67n, 71n, 213

Barnard, Chester I., 93–94, 204n

Barriers, to citizen rule, 32–35, 38–39, 41–42

Bay, Christian, 35

Beliefs. See Attitudes; Norms

Benefits, of policies, 130–31, 137

Bentham, J., 36n

Berlin, Isaiah, 49, 50, 51n

Birch, A. H., 9n, 11n–12n, 34, 58n

Blau, Peter M., 7, 131n, 150, 165n, 205n

Board influence, 79, 94–95, 104–15 passim, 165–73 passim

Breton, Albert, 64n, 68n, 207n, 211n

Budgets, 4, 81, 172–73, 179–81

Bureaucrats: attitudes of, 24–26, 85–120, 149–90, 196, 209–10; autonomous, 16, 92–101, 103, 107, 116, 120, 146–47; control concepts of, 107–8, 109–10, 111–13; goal conflicts reconciled by, 82–83; on map (idealized perspective), 16–17; self-control by, 18, 19n, 23–24; in study, 89–92 (see also under Education; Fire department; Housing authority). See also Resistance, by bureaucrats

Calhoun, John C., 36n, 50, 136n

Centralized strategy, with goal conflict, 9, 78–80, 83

Certainty, of technology, 136, 138–40. See also Uncertainty

Citizens, 9, 12–13, 16, 19, 52, 90, 197–200, 211; bureaucrats as, 87–88, 92–101; bureaucrats' attitudes toward, 94, 95–99, 104, 105, 111–13, 116–20; competence of, 30–48, 126–34, 166, 168, 175–76, 177–78; conscious preferences of, 129; cooperation by, 133–34, 182–84, 185, 206; intensity of preferences of,

227

education, 167, 180; in environment of goal conflict, 136, 143;
in housing authority, 185, 196;
"sunshine" laws and, 204; technological certainty and, 139
Professionalism, 154n, 164–66
Public. *See* Citizens
Public choice literature, 64n
Public interest, 18, 19n, 21, 176; bureaucrats safeguarding, 115–16,
117; citizen competence in, 35,
36, 41–42, 43, 44, 45, 117; politicians and, 56, 57, 115–56, 117
Putnam, Robert D., 70n, 102–3,
187n, 209–10; on bureaucrats
and citizens, 98n; on bureaucrats and politicians, 104n, 113–
14, 209–10, 211n; on democracy, 87n–88n; on efficiency,
62n; governance model of, 35n;
on politicians, 151n; politics
model of, 35n, 45n

Radical democracy, 37, 43
Rae, Douglas W., 50n
Redevelopment agencies, 147
Redford, Emmette S., 80n, 82n
Red tape, 52n, 72n, 100
Regulatory agencies, 81n, 82, 135,
213
Reissman, Leonard, 154n, 155n
Representative bureaucracy approach, 10n
Resistance, by bureaucrats, 86–88,
101, 116, 149, 151, 188, 195–96,
201, 213; core identity and,
163–71, 188; costs of, 193–94,
203
Resources, 65, 133–34, 193–94,
202–14 passim; technological
certainty in, 139–40; useful control exchanged for, 178–88, 207
Responsibility, 9n, 11, 21, 62n, 64n,
65, 66
Responsiveness, 8, 9n, 11, 61n, 99,
111, 112–13
Review boards, 198. *See also* Advisory boards
Rockman, Bert A., 70n, 150, 187n,
209–10; on bureaucrats and citi-

zens, 97n–98n; on bureaucrats
and clients, 179n; on bureaucrats and politicians, 104n, 114n,
209–10, 211n; on democracy,
87n–88n; governance model of,
35n; politics model of, 35n, 45n
Rourke, Francis E., 61n
Rousseau, Jean-Jacques, 37, 51,
199n

Sabine, George, 49
Sartori, Giovanni, 62n
Scale, of government operations,
33, 39–40
School-community councils, 182–
83, 187, 207
Schubert, Glendon, 42, 43n
Schumpeter, Joseph A., 38n, 128n
Scott, W. Richard, 131n, 165n
Sectoral strategy, with goal conflict,
80–82, 83
Security, job, 155–56, 168n
Self-control, by bureaucrats, 18,
19n, 23–24
Self-governance, by citizens, 32–47,
85, 96, 125–27, 132. *See also* De-
mocracy
Selznick, Philip, 81n
Service agencies, 131n, 135
Social security, environment of,
125n
Social Security Administration, 58,
66n, 200–201
Sovereignty, popular, 37, 49
Specialization, technological, 138,
140–41, 142, 153, 195
Spending cuts, government, 4, 81.
See also Budgets
Spiro, Herbert J., 11n, 64n
Staffing policies, public control
through, 10
Staff professional, identity as, 162–
63
Stevenson, C. L., 9n
Stout, Russell, Jr., 63n, 214n
Structural barriers, to citizen rule,
33, 35, 38–39, 41
Substance, 13–22 passim, 48–49,
54, 73, 135, 192, 202; core iden-
tity related to, 153–70 passim; in

Compositor: Wilsted & Taylor
Text: 11/13 Baskerville
Display: Baskerville
Printer: Braun-Brumfield
Binder: Braun-Brumfield